MATT AND TOM OLDFIELD

CLASSIC
FOOTBALL HEROES

GIGGS

FROM THE PLAYGROUND
TO THE PITCH

DINO

Published by Dino Books
an imprint of John Blake Publishing Ltd
3 Bramber Court, 2 Bramber Road,
London W14 9PB, England

www.johnblakepublishing.com

www.facebook.com/johnblakebooks ![]
twitter.com/jblakebooks ![]

First published in paperback in 2017

ISBN: 978 1 78606 805 7

British Library Cataloguing-in-Publication Data:

A catalogue record for this book is available from the British Library.

Design by www.envydesign.co.uk
Cover illustration by Dan Leydon
Background image: Shutterstock

Printed in Great Britain by CPI Group (UK) Ltd

1 3 5 7 9 10 8 6 4 2

Papers used by John Blake Publishing are natural, recyclable products made from
wood grown in sustainable forests. The manufacturing processes conform to the
environmental regulations of the country of origin.

Every attempt has been made to contact the relevant copyright-holders, but some
were unobtainable. We would be grateful if the appropriate people could contact us.

John Blake Publishing is an imprint of Bonnier Publishing
www.bonnierpublishing.co.uk

For Noah and the future Oldfields to come

Looking forward to reading this book together

CLASSIC FOOTBALL HEROES

Matt Oldfield is an accomplished writer and the editor-in-chief of football review site Of Pitch & Page. Tom Oldfield is a freelance sports writer and the author of biographies on Cristiano Ronaldo, Arsène Wenger and Rafael Nadal.

Cover illustration by Dan Leydon.
To learn more about Dan visit danleydon.com
To purchase his artwork visit etsy.com/shop/footynews
Or just follow him on Twitter @danleydon

TABLE OF CONTENTS

ACKNOWLEDGEMENTS

First of all, I'd like to thank John Blake Publishing –
and particularly my editor James Hodgkinson – for
giving me the opportunity to work on these books
and for supporting me throughout. Writing stories for
the next generation of football fans is both an honour
and a pleasure.

I wouldn't be doing this if it wasn't for Tom. I owe
him so much and I'm very grateful for his belief in
me as an author. I feel like Robin setting out on a
solo career after a great partnership with Batman. I
hope I do him (Tom, not Batman) justice with these
new books.

Next up, I want to thank my friends for keeping

me sane during long hours in front of the laptop. Pang, Will, Mills, Doug, John, Charlie – the laughs and the cups of coffee are always appreciated.

I've already thanked my brother but I'm also very grateful to the rest of my family, especially Melissa, Noah and of course Mum and Dad. To my parents, I owe my biggest passions: football and books. They're a real inspiration for everything I do.

Finally, I couldn't have done this without Iona's encouragement and understanding during long, work-filled weekends. Much love to you.

CHAPTER 1

LEAVING AS A LEGEND

From the touchline, Ryan looked up at the Old Trafford scoreboard:

'Manchester United 2 Hull 1 – 67 minutes'

After so many years at United as a player, it felt very strange to now be the manager of the club. But Ryan was determined to carry on the amazing work that his hero and father figure, Sir Alex Ferguson, had started more than twenty-five years earlier.

'We've got two aims,' he liked to tell the players. 'We want to win trophies and play entertaining football.'

Like Fergie with the famous 'Class of '92', Ryan put his trust in youth and it was working well. On his debut, young striker James Wilson had scored two brilliant goals to put United ahead. Sometimes, youngsters just needed an opportunity and a supportive manager.

'It's time,' Ryan said to himself and he began warming up along the touchline. When the fans noticed, they began to sing:

Ryan Giggs, Ryan Giggs,
Running down the wing,
Ryan Giggs, Ryan Giggs,
Running down the wing.
Feared by the Blues,
Loved by the Reds,
Ryan Giggs, Ryan Giggs, Ryan Giggs!

Ryan got goosebumps as he listened but he stayed focused on the game. After doing his stretches, he took off his tracksuit. Wearing the Number 11 shirt, he was ready to make his final appearance.

'Good luck!' Steve Bruce, the Hull manager said, patting him on the back. Back in the 1990s, they had been teammates together at United. They had shared many happy times and many trophies.

The whole stadium clapped as Ryan ran on to the pitch. He was not only a United legend, but a Premier League legend too. Somehow at forty years old, he was still good enough to play at the highest level. He no longer had the incredible speed that had made him a wing wizard and he couldn't play as many games as he used to, but he still had the talent to create moments of magic.

'I'll take it,' Ryan said when United won a free kick and no-one argued with him. This was his day and he was their manager.

He took a deep breath. It was probably his last chance to score a goal in front of the amazing United fans, so he had to get it right. He curled the ball with his left foot, just like he had so many times before. Everyone in the crowd held their breath as it flew towards the top corner.

Ooooooooooooooooooooooooooooooooooohhhhhh-hhhhhhhhhhhhhhhhhhhhhhhhh

But the Hull goalkeeper made a brilliant save to

tip it round the post. The crowd groaned. Ryan put his hands to his head – 'So close!' he said to Michael Carrick.

The match ended 3-1 to United. At the final whistle, Ryan shook hands with the referee and the Hull players. A good sportsman didn't just play well; he was also polite and respectful to others.

After hugging his teammates, he couldn't put it off any longer. It was time for Ryan to speak to the fans. With a microphone in his hand and thousands of faces watching him, he felt just as shy as he had as a thirteen-year-old arriving at Manchester United for the first time.

'Thank you for your support this year,' he began and already he could feel the tears coming. He wiped his eyes. 'We know it's been tough this season but I'm sure that in the coming years we'll bring you more success.'

Ryan Giggs' Red Army! Ryan Giggs' Red Army!

Would the fans always chant his name? He really hoped so.

'Keep supporting us and the good times will come back soon!'

The crowd roared and Ryan sent the players on a lap of honour around Old Trafford. It was a very emotional day. After twenty-four seasons in the United first team, Ryan was finally hanging up his boots.

As he walked around the stadium, clapping to the fans, he thought back on all of his amazing memories at the club: winning the FA Youth Cup with Becks, Scholesy, Nicky, Gary and Phil; winning a record thirteen Premier League titles; winning four FA Cup trophies; winning four League Cup trophies; and winning two Champions League trophies.

Ryan was the greatest winner in the history of British football. As a teenager, he had dazzled with his pace and dribbling skills but as he grew older, he won matches with his vision and intelligence. United would never have another wing wizard like Ryan – he was unique.

The club had been his home for most of his life. With the support of Sir Alex Ferguson and the United coaches, he had grown from 'the next big thing' to become the Premier League's most successful player.

Ryan had enjoyed every minute of his amazing football adventure. And it had all started on the streets of Cardiff, Wales.

CHAPTER 2

KING OF
CARDIFF

'Ryan! Ryan!'

He could hear his grandma calling his name from
their house nearby but he wasn't quite finished.
Besides, she knew the rule – a match never finished
until it was too dark to see.

Ryan won the ball one last time and dribbled at his
opponents. He knew that he could beat them all – he
had way too much pace and skill for them. He went
past one tired tackle, then another and then another,
weaving from right to left. In winter, there wasn't
much grass left on their pitch and there were lots
of obstacles like rocks and drink cans. But for Ryan,

dribbling past defenders was as easy as going round cones on a training pitch.

His teammates had stopped running to watch his skills. Ryan was a wizard with the ball at his feet and they knew that he was never going to pass. He still didn't have much power in his little legs but the only way to end his wonder run was to score a wonder goal. He shot low and hard with his left foot and the ball flew past the goalkeeper's dive and off into the far corner of the field.

'Coming!' Ryan finally shouted, loud enough for his grandma to hear. It was time to celebrate with a lovely big dinner. He was starving.

'Hey! You've got to get the ball back first!' Chris shouted but Ryan was already running away. Chris and Ryan were good friends, but Ryan's habit of scoring the winner and running off without fetching the ball never failed to annoy him.

'Fine, well we'll stick you in goal tomorrow!' Chris threatened as he watched Ryan go inside his house. 'The teams are never fair when you play anyway.'

It was true. Whichever team Ryan played for would always win. He was the best player by a mile and all of the other boys were jealous of his talent. He was a natural.

'How did it go?' his grandpa Dennis asked as they sat down to eat together. Ryan's younger brother, Rhodri, had already had his dinner and was playing with his toys on the carpet.

Dennis was a big football fan and always wanted to know about his grandson's matches. It was his dream to have a professional footballer in the family, and he had seen that – even at the age of five – Ryan had lots of potential.

'What are you doing inside on a day like this?' Dennis said if his grandson looked bored in the house. 'Go out and play with your friends!'

With his parents working hard, Ryan spent a lot of time with his grandparents. They were the best babysitters ever.

'I scored so many goals that I lost count!' Ryan said proudly as he wolfed down a plate of sausages, mashed potato and peas.

'That's my boy!' Dennis replied with a wink. 'You've certainly got your dad's gift for sports.'

Ryan's dad Danny was a professional rugby player for Cardiff RFC. Danny ran really fast with the ball to escape tackles, just like Ryan did on the football pitch. In Wales, rugby was the biggest sport but players didn't earn as much money as footballers. So even though his dad was a national hero and his mum juggled two jobs, they still couldn't afford to buy a house of their own. Ryan didn't mind, though. He loved living with his grandparents.

'And how was school?' his grandma, Margaret, asked.

'At lunch-time we played against the older boys and we won,' Ryan answered excitedly in between massive mouthfuls. 'Gareth Jones is in the year above and he says that he's going to ask the coach if I can play for the school team!'

His grandma laughed. 'That's great but I meant how were your classes? What did you learn today?'

'Oh right, the classes were fine,' Ryan said. Suddenly he was quiet again. He didn't want to talk about his lessons. He wasn't a naughty boy but he wasn't that interested in learning new things – unless they were cool football tricks, of course.

'How are you doing with the national anthem?' Dennis asked with a big smile on his face. He liked to tease his grandson. 'Let's hear you sing it before you get your pudding!'

Every morning at Hwyel Dda Primary School, Ryan had to sing the Welsh national anthem. It was his least favourite part of the day because he didn't understand a single word of the Welsh language.

'No way!' Ryan replied, shaking his head. He was a shy boy and he wasn't going to embarrass himself to make his grandpa laugh.

'Well then I guess there's no pudding for you!' his grandma joined in but a few seconds later, Ryan was tucking into a big bowl of jelly and ice cream. They loved to spoil him.

As they cleared the table, Ryan's mum came home from work.

'How's the next John Toshack?' Lynne asked, giving her son a big hug.

John Toshack was his mum's favourite footballer.
He was a striker who played for Liverpool and Wales,
and he scored lots of goals. Because of his dad, Ryan
played rugby too but he loved football much more.
Kids didn't play rugby in the streets; they played
football. It was way more fun.

'I scored lots more goals today!' Ryan told his
mum. 'You should have seen the last one – I ran past
everyone!'

'Well done! And how was school?'

'Why does everyone ask me about school?' Ryan
complained. 'I don't want to talk about boring things!'

CHAPTER 3

MOVING TO MANCHESTER

'Where's Ryan?' Danny asked as he got home from rugby training one day. Lynne was looking after their younger son, Rhodri, in the kitchen.

'Listen,' she replied, rolling her eyes.

Smack! Smack! Smack!

Danny followed the sounds and looked out of the window. Ryan was kicking a football against the side of the house again and again, first with his left foot and then with his right foot.

'He's been doing that for hours,' Lynne said. 'That wall's going to fall down soon!'

'At least he's not doing it inside,' Danny laughed.

'I sent him outside because he was kicking the radiator instead!'

It was impossible for Ryan to keep still. He was a quiet child but his feet made plenty of noise. With most things, he got bored very quickly but for some reason, he could kick a ball back and forth all day long without losing focus.

'Ryan, stop that and come in here!' his dad called out of the window.

'Right, I have some big news,' Danny said once everyone was sitting around the table. 'I've had a great offer to go and play for a team called Swinton RLFC.'

'Who are they?' Ryan asked straight away. He had never heard of them and they didn't sound Welsh. He didn't like the sound of them at all.

'They're a Rugby League side in Manchester,' his dad replied.

'Where's that?' Ryan asked.

'It's in England,' Lynne explained. She knew that her sons would be very upset about the big move. It was a huge decision to make but it was a very good job. Danny couldn't say no.

'How often will you be able to come back to Wales and visit us, Dad?' Ryan asked next. He was still in denial.

His mum frowned. 'No son, we'll all be going to Manchester too.'

It took another minute for Ryan to really understand what that meant but soon the tears were streaming down his face.

'No, I don't want to go! All my friends are here!'

'Son, you'll make new friends in Manchester,' his dad tried to explain but it was no use. Ryan was six years old and this was the worst news that he had ever heard.

'I don't want new friends. I'm staying here with Grandma and Grandpa!'

'You'll be able to talk to them on the phone all the time. And you can come back to visit in the holidays,' Lynne suggested, hoping that this might calm her son down.

Ryan ran off to his bedroom and slammed the door. He loved his life in Cardiff – his local school, his home, his grandparents, and especially the football pitch next door. He didn't want everything to change. He didn't want to start again in a new place.

It was very difficult saying goodbye. Margaret cried and cried as her family packed their belongings into the car. She would miss her grandsons so much. As they drove off towards England, Ryan looked out of the back window and waved and waved until his grandparents were long out of sight. He was dreading his new adventure.

'This place is rubbish!' Ryan said to Rhodri when they arrived at their new home. It was in a nice, safe neighbourhood and there was even an apple tree in the front garden.

'I don't think it's that bad,' his younger brother bravely replied.

'Shut up!' Ryan said, throwing an apple at him. 'Where can we play football?'

They played two-touch for a bit outside the house, standing on the pavements either side of the road. But every time a car came past, the game had to stop.

'This is ridiculous!' Ryan moaned. He wished that he was back on the field in Pentrebane next to his grandparents' house. There was plenty of space to play there and no traffic to get in the way.

As he watched the local kids riding by on their bikes, Ryan had a naughty idea. The next time a group went past, he started throwing apples at them. Soon, their front garden was the scene of a big apple war.

Get them!

Keep throwing more!

It was chaos. Ryan and Rhodri were outnumbered but they fought hard to protect their territory. They laughed and cheered as they ducked and swerved. It was great fun until they got caught.

'What on earth is going on out here?' Danny shouted, as he stormed out of the front door.

Uh-oh! Suddenly, Rhodri looked very worried. They were in big trouble and it was all his big brother's fault. The whole street was covered in crushed apples. It was an absolute mess and their dad was furious. He was very scary when he got angry. He was a big rugby player, after all.

'This is our first day here and you're already misbehaving,' he boomed. 'Clear this up immediately!'

The other kids had run away as fast as they could

and so Ryan and Rhodri spent hours cleaning up on their own. It was worth it, though. At least they had made some new friends.

There was also another way that Ryan made new friends: football. After the apple war, the local kids invited him to come and play with them and Ryan quickly showed them how good he was.

'You Welsh boyos prefer rugby, don't you?' Neil joked before the game started. 'Wales are rubbish at football!'

Ryan didn't say anything – he would let his feet do the talking. As soon as he got the ball, he dribbled forward and set up a goal. Nobody could tackle him. After running rings around the others for a few hours, the teasing quickly stopped.

'Maybe we were wrong about Welsh footballers!' Neil laughed. Thanks to Ryan, they had thrashed their opponents.

Ryan was one of the boys now. He was the player that everyone wanted to play with, and nobody wanted to play against.

CHAPTER 4

OLD TRAFFORD

'Have you been good boys today?' Danny asked one evening at dinner.

Ryan and Rhodri both nodded straight away. Their mum Lynne was smiling so it didn't seem like they were in trouble. Ryan hoped that maybe his dad had a treat for them.

'Good, because I've got something you might be interested in.'

Danny reached into his shirt pocket and pulled out three tickets – 'Manchester United vs Ipswich Town'.

A huge smile spread across Ryan's face. At the age of eight, this would be his first ever trip to Old Trafford. He had been hoping to go to the 'Theatre of

Dreams' ever since the family arrived in Manchester. Now, it was finally going to happen.

Ryan had grown up as a United fan because of his grandma Margaret. Living in Wales, she had fallen in love with the famous 'Busby Babes' team of the 1950s, and United legend George Best was her favourite ever player. Margaret had made sure that there was only one team that her grandsons were going to support.

'Amazing – thanks Dad! Do you think Mickey Thomas will be playing?'

Mickey Thomas was Ryan's favourite player for three reasons. 1) He was Welsh, just like Ryan. 2) He was a left-footed midfielder, just like Ryan. 3) He played for Manchester United, Ryan's favourite team. Seeing Mickey Thomas live would be a dream come true.

Ryan was so excited as they arrived at Old Trafford. With his red hat and red scarf, he was ready to cheer on his heroes. The stadium looked so much bigger than the rugby stadiums where he watched his dad play.

'How many people will there be inside?' Ryan asked.

'Nearly 50,000,' Danny answered.

The number was too big for Ryan to even imagine. As they went in, his dad bought a programme to get the all-important team news.

'Your hero is starting!' Danny said, pointing at a name on the page – 'Mickey Thomas'.

'Yes!' Ryan said, punching the air with joy.

As they took their seats, they stared out at the incredible scene. It was hard to take in the sheer size of everything: the rows and rows of seats all around them and the massive pitch below. The match hadn't even started and already the fans were singing songs about their heroes. Ryan loved the buzz in the air.

'Imagine if we got to play football here one day,' he said to his brother, Rhodri.

'Well that pitch doesn't look much better than the ones you play on every Sunday!' their dad joked. It had been raining all day and there was mud everywhere.

When Ipswich took the lead, Ryan feared the worst.

He wanted to see his team win, not lose. With the ball getting stuck in the mud, Mickey Thomas couldn't show off his brilliant skills.

'Come on, Mickey!' Ryan shouted.

United attacked down the left wing and their striker had a shot at goal. The goalkeeper made a good save but the ball bounced out. Before a defender could make a clearance, Mickey Thomas came running into the penalty area and smashed the ball into the net.

Ryan couldn't believe it – in his first game at Old Trafford, he had watched his hero score! It was even better than he had hoped it would be. His dad lifted him high into the air so that he could see the celebrations on the pitch. Ryan cheered and cheered – it was an amazing moment.

United! United! United!

In the second half, Manchester United won the game thanks to a brilliant Jimmy Nicholl strike. Again, the crowd went wild and Ryan was right at the centre of it all. The atmosphere was electric. It was the perfect end to a perfect day.

'What a game! Dad, can we go again soon please?' Ryan asked on the way home.

'Yes, can we?' Rhodri pleaded.

'I'll see what I can do but it's very difficult to get tickets,' Danny replied. 'So did you enjoy today?'

'United! United! United!' the brothers shouted together.

Their dad laughed. 'I'll take that as a yes!'

CHAPTER 5

DEANS F.C.

'How are you doing, Ryan?' Margaret asked on the phone one night. 'We haven't heard much from you lately. We miss you!'

'Sorry, Grandma!' he replied guiltily. When he first arrived in Manchester, Ryan used to call his grandparents all the time and visit them back in Wales almost every weekend. But his life had become very busy lately and he hadn't eaten one of his grandma's amazing Sunday roasts in months. 'I'm playing a lot of sport now.'

His grandma laughed. 'I had a feeling that sport might be the reason!'

At first Ryan's life was just football, football and

more football. If he wasn't playing it in the fields near their house, he was playing it in the playground at Grosvenor Road Primary School. There was no limit to Ryan's energy and his love for the beautiful game.

But the sports teacher at Grosvenor Road, Robert Mason, preferred rugby and he knew all about Ryan's dad.

'I've seen your dad play rugby and I've seen you play football,' Mason told him. 'You've got the same speed, the same running style and the same balance as you change direction. Like father, like son! I know how much you love football but there's no reason why you can't play rugby too.'

Ryan had learnt a lot about rugby league from watching his dad play at Swinton. He found the sport very easy and soon he was playing four matches of sport every weekend: football on Saturday mornings and Sunday afternoons, and rugby on Saturday afternoons and Sunday mornings. By each Sunday night, he was exhausted but happy.

'I'm surprised you can even lift your knife and fork!' Lynne joked as Ryan wolfed down his dinner.

Although he worked as a milkman during the day, Dennis Schofield's passion was for football. He was the coach of one of the best Sunday League teams in the Manchester area, Deans F.C. When Dennis wasn't watching his own sides play, he was looking out for new talents in other matches. If there was a football game going on, he couldn't help but stop and watch.

One day, he was driving past the Grosvenor Road school, when he spotted a match kicking off. Dennis parked his van and walked over to the touchline. 'You never know what you might see,' he said to himself.

It certainly wasn't the best football he had ever seen but a young kid on the left wing really caught his eye. Most of the game was happening in the centre of the pitch, where the kids ran around like headless chickens, chasing the ball. But when the ball did eventually make it out to the left, the winger took his opportunity brilliantly. He ran straight at the right back, using his pace and skill to fool him. Another defender came across to tackle him but he had no chance. The winger pretended to dribble one way but then went the other.

'Go on, kid!' Dennis found himself shouting.

As the winger ran towards the penalty area, he looked up and saw his striker waiting. He put a brilliant cross into the box and the striker had a simple tap-in to score. Dennis's excitement grew and grew as the winger did it again and again. Dennis had never seen such a skilful performance from someone so young. The kid seemed to be a few years ahead of all of the other players on the pitch. By the final whistle, the defenders had given up.

Dennis crossed the pitch to talk to the wing wizard. 'Well played, kid. That was amazing! What's your name?'

'Ryan Wilson,' he replied.

'It's very nice to meet you, Ryan! My name is Dennis Schofield and I run a great local football team called Deans F.C. I want you to come down and play for us. What do you think about that?'

'That sounds great!' Ryan said. He was waiting for his mum to pick him up but he knew that his parents would be happy to see him playing for a proper team and using up more of his energy.

'Brilliant! We've got a game on Sunday – do you want to play?'

'Sure, but don't I need to come and train with the team first?' Ryan asked. What if the other players were amazing and he embarrassed himself?

'Don't worry, you'll be fine. Give me your address and I'll collect you and take you home afterwards too,' Dennis said.

As he entered the changing room before his first match, Ryan could hear lots of laughter. That was a good sign and it calmed his nerves.

'Hey, aren't you Danny's son?' Simon, one of his new teammates, asked when he was introduced.

'Yes,' Ryan replied shyly. Sometimes it was difficult having a famous dad.

'That's so cool – he's an amazing rugby player!'

'What position do you play?' Stuart, another teammate, asked. Ryan spotted his football boots straight away – they were brand new and must have cost a fortune. 'He must be good,' Ryan thought to himself.

'Left wing.'

'Cool, I play in central midfield,' Stuart told him.
'It's going to be a hard game today but just do your
best and make lots of attacking runs.'

Ryan nodded eagerly – that's what he did best.

Stuart was right – it was a *really* hard game. Their
opponents, Stretford Victoria, were the best team
in the area and they scored goal after goal. On the
wing, Ryan hardly ever got the ball but when he did,
he tried to show off his tricks. He was desperate to
impress his new teammates but it was an awful debut.

As the match ended and the teams shook hands,
Ryan was gutted. He had never lost like that before. It
was his chance to shine and he had failed.

'You were unlucky today, lads,' Dennis said, trying
to lift the dropped heads. 'They're an excellent side
and you worked really hard to stop them. Well done
– we'll get back to winning ways next week. There's
no doubt in my mind about today's man of the match.
Ryan, congratulations on a great debut!'

As everyone clapped, Ryan couldn't believe it. He
thought he had played one of his worst games ever.
Were they all watching a different match?

'Ryan, you've got to come back next week – we need you!' Stuart begged as they said goodbye.

'I didn't think you'd want me after that defeat!' Ryan laughed. 'I'll help us win next time, I promise.'

CHAPTER 6

BIG
DECISIONS

'Have you made up your mind yet?' his grandpa asked
Ryan every time he came to visit. 'Which sport are
you going to choose – rugby or football?'

By the age of thirteen, it was definitely time for
Ryan to decide. In rugby, he had been picked to play
for the county of Lancashire after a trial. He was also
playing football for Lancashire and the coaches said
that if he kept improving, he would soon be playing
for Great Britain.

'I can't believe you're complaining about this,' his
friend and Deans teammate Simon joked. 'Poor you,
the natural sportsman!'

Ryan laughed. It was a nice problem to have but it was still a problem. He decided to talk to his dad about it.

'Son, you should play whichever sport you enjoy more,' was Danny's reply. He never wanted to push Ryan to follow in his rugby footsteps.

'I still find rugby easier than football but I don't know if I'm big enough,' Ryan explained.

'It's not all about size,' his dad replied. 'You've watched me enough times to know that it's mostly about skill!'

'I know, and I'm still the quickest player but the other boys keep getting stronger and stronger and I'm still pretty skinny. The other day, I got tackled by a kid that was twice as wide as me and I could hardly breathe!'

Danny smiled. 'Okay, imagine that you got an injury that meant you could only play one game of sport each week for the rest of your life. Which would you choose?'

Ryan thought long and hard about his dad's question. Which sport did all of his mates play? Which sport did he love most? Finally, he made his big decision. 'Football.'

* * *

A few weeks later at the end of a Deans training session, Dennis Schofield called Ryan and Stuart over.

'I've got some big news, boys,' he began. 'On Thursday, you're coming to train with Manchester City!'

Dennis worked as a scout for the club and he was only taking his best young players. Ryan was really pleased to be selected but there was one big drawback: he supported City's local rivals, Manchester United.

'Wow, congratulations!' Lynne said when Ryan told her. 'Have you told your grandma yet? She won't be happy!'

Margaret was a huge United fan and if there was one team that she didn't want her grandson playing for, it was City. That was unthinkable.

'Are you sure you want to wear that?' Stuart asked

when Ryan got into the car to go to training. Stuart was wearing a plain black football kit but Ryan had decided to wear red, the colour of United.

'It's the only shirt I have that's clean,' Ryan lied.

'You're either very brave or very stupid!' Dennis laughed.

The Manchester City youth team practised on astroturf rather than grass. Ryan hated it because when he tried to turn with the ball, he slipped. Great balance was key to his dribbling style and so it was a nightmare. And things got even worse when the coaches spotted his shirt.

'Kid, you're not a Red, are you?' one of them asked.

He looked like he was joking but Ryan couldn't be sure. He kept quiet.

'You'll need to wear this,' the coach said, handing him a bright orange bib. 'That colour just isn't allowed around here.'

Ryan did his best in the training match but he didn't feel comfortable at the club. How could he play football for the enemies of his favourite club?

'Did you enjoy that?' Dennis asked at the end. He could see that Ryan wasn't his usual happy self.

'Yeah, it was okay,' he replied.

City were very impressed with Ryan's talent and they asked him to return. Eric Mullender, their scout, took him under his wing and gave him a club tracksuit.

'You've got a very bright future here,' Eric told him. 'In a few years, you could be wearing that for the first team!'

Ryan was grateful for his support but he couldn't get used to wearing blue. It just didn't feel right. He played a few matches for City but until he turned fourteen, Ryan couldn't sign a contract that tied him to a particular club. And luckily, City weren't the only team that were interested. So were Preston, so were Liverpool – and so were Manchester United, largely thanks to Harold Wood.

CHAPTER 7

UNITED

Harold Wood worked as a newsagent but football was what he loved the most. As a steward at Old Trafford, he watched his beloved Manchester United whenever they played at home, while on the pitches near his house, he watched his other favourite team – the local youth side, Deans F.C.

Whatever the weather, Harold was always out there on the sidelines. He loved watching young talent and Deans had one of the best he had ever seen – a left winger called Ryan Wilson. When the ball was at his feet, Ryan came alive. He loved to create goals and he made it look so easy. He had the pace to glide straight past defenders, and the dribbling skills to leave them dazed and confused. Again and again, Deans thrashed their opponents and it was largely thanks to Ryan. Harold was sure that the kid was ready to play at a much higher level.

'Have you been down to see Ryan Wilson yet?' he would ask the Manchester United youth scouts when he saw them at Old Trafford. 'Trust me; he's better than any player that you've got at the academy right now.'

'You never give up, do you?' they replied with a smile but they still wouldn't listen to him. So in the end, Harold decided to speak to the manager about it.

'I'm sorry to bother you but I've seen a youngster that I really think you should take a look at,' he said when he finally got to talk to Alex Ferguson. 'He plays for Deans F.C. and Salford Boys, and he's training at City at the moment. But he's a Red! He's a tricky left winger like George Best.'

Ferguson had heard so many kids compared to the Manchester United legend but he listened to Harold.

'Thanks, I'll get someone to go down to watch his next match.'

'Terrific – you won't regret it!'

Eric Harrison was the United youth coach who
went to watch Ryan play for Deans. The first thing
he noticed was the boy's long legs and his dribbling
style. He seemed to glide his way across the pitch
like it was an ice rink, and it was a beautiful thing
to watch. Eric had been watching young players
for years and he had seen some of Britain's best
ever talents. But Ryan completely took his breath
away.

'I've never seen a kid play like that,' he told Fergie
on the phone as soon as the game was over. 'We have
to do whatever it takes to sign him!'

Ryan was the captain of Salford Boys when they
came to Manchester United's training ground, 'The
Cliff', for a match against the club's Under-15s.
United had some of the best youngsters in not just
Manchester but the whole of England, especially Nick
Barmby and Raphael Burke. But Ryan wasn't scared;
he couldn't wait for the challenge.

'Come on boys, these players think they're the best
around,' he told his teammates before kick-off to get

them ready for the big game. 'Let's show them who's boss around here!'

It was the one and only game that Ryan ever wanted United to lose. He was determined to show their coaches just how good he could be.

Ferguson thought he'd watch the first few minutes of the game from his office window but soon he couldn't take his eyes off the action. He'd expected United to dominate the match but it was quite the opposite. Salford were on top thanks to their brilliant left winger. Fergie would never forget the star he saw that day.

The United defenders tried to stop Ryan again and again but he twisted and turned his way past them all. He could shift his balance from one side to the other so quickly that opponents had no idea which way he was going. It was so exciting to watch. And once he had the space, the winger was lightning-quick, running towards goal like a dog chasing a ball. Not only could the kid dribble and cross, but he could also score. By the final whistle, he had a hat-trick.

'Wow, so that's the Ryan Wilson that the steward

was telling me about!' Ferguson laughed to himself. He owed Harold Wood big time – he had discovered a real gem.

Ryan was very happy with his performance and he had no idea that Ferguson was watching. His opponents were certainly impressed.

'You're exactly what our team needs!' Raphael said as they shook hands at the end. 'I'm sure our defenders will pay you just to make sure they don't have to play against you again.'

'If United don't want to sign you after that, then you might as well retire!' Stuart joked. He was really pleased for his friend. He knew how much it would mean to him to play for his favourite club.

Ferguson spoke with his coaches and soon Ryan was offered a trial at Manchester United. The dream was actually coming true! He couldn't wait to tell everyone the great news, but there was one person in particular that he knew would be delighted.

'Grandma, guess who I'll be training with next week?' Ryan asked excitedly on the phone that evening.

'Never! Are you teasing me?' Margaret replied. She was over the moon. 'My grandson is going to be a Red!'

'It's only a trial, Grandma!'

'There's no way that they'll let you go now,' she said confidently. 'You're the next George Best!'

CHAPTER 8

ON THE RISE

'Do you think Manchester United are going to sign you?'

'Is it true that other clubs are offering you lots of money?'

As his fourteenth birthday approached, Ryan's friends kept asking him what he would do next. Their mate had the chance to become a famous superstar and that was really exciting for all of them. Ryan's answer was simple and always the same:

'If United want me, then there's no way I'm going anywhere else!'

Other teams tried to tempt him with thousands of pounds or a year's supply of football boots, but all he wanted was to keep playing for the club that he loved.

Like City, United trained on astroturf but there the similarities ended. As soon as Ryan arrived at his first training session, he felt at home. Scout Joe Brown showed him around the facilities at 'The Cliff' and introduced him to the Head of Youth Development.

'Ryan, this is Brian Kidd,' Joe said. 'He's the best coach around – if there's anything you need, just let him know.'

Brian had a very firm handshake. 'Welcome to the club, Ryan. I've been hearing a lot about you over the last few weeks. If you work hard and want to learn, we'll get on really well and we'll make you a better player.'

Brian made it sound so easy but Ryan had never been so nervous. The practices were fun but really challenging. He had gone from being a giant fish in a small pond to a tiny fish in the biggest pond he'd ever seen. At first, Ryan watched Nick and Raphael's skills and worried that he couldn't compete.

'There's no way I'll ever be as good as them!' he moaned to his mum when he got home.

'Nonsense!' Lynne replied immediately. She was so proud of her son but he needed to share her confidence in his ability. 'Remember what Brian told you? "Work hard and want to learn" – listen to that advice and believe in yourself.'

Soon, Ryan was back to being a big fish again. His natural talent and fast learning was a winning combination for the United coaches. They taught him about tactics and decision-making but they also encouraged him to keep trying new things.

'When you've got space in front of you on the wing, just do what you normally do!' they told him. There was no point trying to change something that worked so well.

On his fourteenth birthday, Ryan went to play football in the park with his friends just like he did on any other day. Only, it wasn't any other day. It was only when he came home and saw the big, gold Mercedes car parked outside that he remembered what was happening.

'Oh no!' he shouted. 'How did I forget that Alex Ferguson was coming to my house?!'

'I'm in such big trouble!' he thought to himself as he crept quietly through the front door.

'I think that must be Ryan now,' he heard his mum say. She sounded much more formal than normal. 'Ryan!'

As he walked into the living room, he saw Joe Brown and Alex Ferguson happily drinking tea. They had been counting down the days until they could finally sign Ryan to a proper contract. It had been a long wait but they knew that the kid was worth it.

Ryan might have forgotten the meeting was taking place but there was no way he would ever forget the sight of the Manchester United manager sitting in his home. It was hard to believe.

'Do we not give you enough football training at "The Cliff"?' Ferguson joked. 'I thought you'd take a day off for your birthday!'

Ryan smiled but he felt very shy. His heart was beating so fast in his chest. This was the moment that he'd always dreamed of but suddenly, he wanted it to be over as quickly as possible. Luckily, Ferguson got straight down to business.

'Ryan, we truly believe that you're going to be a massive part of the future of this club,' he said, handing over the form to sign. 'This is the two-year associate schoolboy deal but we're very confident that you'll turn professional in three years.'

'Professional' – Ryan loved the sound of that word. 'Professional footballer' sounded even better. 'Professional footballer for Manchester United' was out of this world.

* * *

'Dennis, the cameras are on Ryan!' Margaret shouted and her husband came rushing into the room as quickly as he could.

Salford Boys had made it all the way to the Granada Schools Cup Final and that meant a trip to Liverpool's famous stadium, Anfield, as well as an appearance on TV. Ryan should have been playing for the United Under-15s at Old Trafford instead but he couldn't miss Salford's big day. He was playing with some of his best mates and he was the captain. Before kick-off, commentator Martin Tyler told the TV viewers about the star player:

Ryan Wilson is a major influence on the Salford team. He's on Manchester United's books.

'That's my boy!' Dennis cheered at the screen.

Ryan was wearing the green Number 6 shirt and he looked very calm as he passed the ball around and stretched his legs.

Salford started well but it was their opponents Blackburn who took the lead. Ryan knew that he needed to do better for his team. On such a massive pitch, his pace could be so important. They were relying on him to be their match-winner.

'Come on boys, this isn't over!' he shouted in the changing room at half-time.

In the second-half, Ryan got the ball in his own half and ran forward. He beat the first defender with ease.

That's a good turn by Wilson. He's on to his stronger left side and he's stretching away now...

'Go on Ryan!' Margaret screamed.

Just before he reached the edge of the pitch, Ryan crossed the ball into the danger area. The defender panicked and sliced his clearance and the goalkeeper could only deflect it into his own net. 1-1 – Salford were back in the game thanks to Ryan.

But after some poor defending, Blackburn scored a second. Ryan would need to do it all again. As he picked the ball up around the centre-circle, there were three opponents chasing him but they couldn't keep up. With all eyes on him, the defenders had missed Darren Winwood's great run into the box. But Ryan hadn't. Just when it looked like he might get tackled, he chipped a perfect ball through and Darren made it 2-2.

...*set up beautifully for him by Ryan Wilson!*

The match went to extra time and there were a lot of tired legs out there. When Ryan got the ball out on the left wing, he had acres of space for dribbling. Defenders tried to stop him but he ran past them easily. Again, all attention was on Ryan and so when he crossed to Darren, he had an easy finish. Finally, Salford were winning.

'We can't make any mistakes now!' Ryan warned his teammates.

It was a great relief when the referee finally blew the final whistle.

Salford, with Wilson outstanding, have won it!

After shaking hands with the Blackburn players, it was celebration time. Ryan led his team up to collect the trophy and their medals. It felt so good to play the man-of-the-match role in the victory. As he raised the trophy into the air, everyone cheered.

On TV, they interviewed Liverpool's chief scout, Ron Yeats. The first question was about Ryan.

'He's something special,' Yeats replied. 'The boy's got pace and he's got skill.'

Ryan was the talk of English football and he was still only fourteen years old.

CHAPTER 9

ENGLAND VS WALES

Ryan didn't usually receive much post, but one morning, a letter arrived for him.

'Maybe it's fan mail!' Rhodri joked but his older brother didn't reply. He was too busy reading the letter, and there was a smile on his face.

'What does it say?' Rhodri asked.

'I've been selected to represent Salford at the England schoolboys trials,' Ryan eventually replied.

'But we're Welsh!' his younger brother argued.

'I know, but it's based on what school you go to, not where you were born,' Ryan explained. 'Moorside High is in England!'

'I know that – I'm not stupid! But would you want

to play for England?' Rhodri continued. 'What about Wales?'

These were questions that Ryan really needed to think about. His Welsh family would not be happy if he ignored his Cardiff roots. But in the meantime, there was no harm in going along to the trials.

When he arrived in Nottingham, Ryan couldn't believe how many other kids were there. How many players did England need?

'This is the start of a very large and long process,' the coaches explained. 'There are over 120 of you here today but we'll be cutting that number down over the next few months. Only eighteen will make it to the final squad.'

Ryan enjoyed the exercises and the matches but he had no idea if he had done enough to make it to the next round. Out on the wing, it was sometimes hard to get involved if all of the action was in the centre of the pitch.

'How did it go?' Rhodri asked Ryan when he got home.

'It was fun but I'm not very confident about my

chances. I didn't really have enough time on the ball to shine.'

'You always say that, though! I bet you were brilliant,' his brother reassured him.

Despite his worries, Ryan made it to the final eighty, then the final forty, then the final twenty-five. Eventually, six months after that first trial, he was named in the final eighteen. And there was still one big final surprise left for him.

'First of all, congratulations on making the England squad!' Dave Bushell, the schoolboys' manager said when he called Ryan into his office for a chat. 'Now to the second thing – we want you to be the captain.'

Ryan couldn't believe it. He was still a shy boy and he never said much on the pitch to encourage his teammates. He seemed a strange choice as leader but he didn't ask why.

'Wow, thanks, it's a massive honour!' he said instead.

The team practised at Lilleshall, at the National Sports Centre. The training facilities were the best that Ryan had ever seen, and the boys were given lots of cool gear – tracksuits, boots, shirts.

'It's worth it just for the free stuff!' he said with a laugh to his brother. The kit was too big for Rhodri but he would grow into it.

As England Schoolboys captain, Ryan was starting to become famous. The British newspapers even printed articles about him, and his family bought as many copies as they could find.

'Stop, it's embarrassing!' he moaned but he was actually very proud. He was 'the next big thing' and that was very exciting.

But when the England Schoolboys matches started, all people seemed to talk about was his nationality. 'So you're English now, are you?' his friends teased. 'I suppose you don't really have a Welsh accent anymore!'

To Ryan, playing for England Schoolboys wasn't the same as playing for England. It was just like playing for Manchester rather than Cardiff.

'I couldn't play for England even if I wanted to,' he tried to explain. 'But I don't want to anyway!'

As soon as he was old enough, Ryan wanted to play for Wales.

'I was born in Wales and all my family are Welsh.

I will always feel Welsh,' he promised his grandma when he went back to Pentrebane for another Sunday roast. Margaret was very happy to hear that.

It was an amazing experience to play at Wembley in front of 50,000 fans, and to score against Germany, but beating Wales was a very weird feeling. Before kick-off, Ryan sang 'God Save the Queen' with the other England boys but he had spent years learning the Welsh anthem, 'Land of my Fathers'. He couldn't help muttering the words under his breath.

All of his family travelled from Cardiff to watch the game at The Vetch Field Stadium in Swansea. There were a lot of mixed loyalties.

'I don't mind you playing this one match against Wales but if you score, there will be trouble!' his grandpa Dennis joked with him before the match.

When he did score, Ryan didn't want to celebrate. He was proud of his home nation and soon enough, he would be playing for them.

'I'm one hundred per cent Welsh. I want to captain my country and I want to be the best footballer they've ever had!'

CHAPTER 10

RYAN GIGGS!

'Ryan, I want you to know that I'm here if you need to talk about anything,' Alex Ferguson said to him one day after training. He could tell that something was wrong with his young superstar.

Fergie liked to be a father figure to all of his young players, but to Ryan in particular. 'When it comes to football, the coaches will help you but if it's something other than football, please come and speak to me.'

Ryan was glad to have such a supportive manager. It was a difficult time for him because his parents had split up. They had always had an up-and-down relationship but now his dad Danny had finally moved out of the family home. Ryan was happy that the arguments were over but he worried about his mum and his brother.

'Thanks boss, that means a lot to me,' he replied.

When Ryan was sixteen, his mum got married. She decided to go back to her maiden name, 'Giggs', and so her sons did the same.

'Are you sure?' Lynne asked Ryan. 'You don't need to do it for me.'

He nodded. 'This is my family – you, Rhodri, and Grandma and Grandpa.'

At first, it was very confusing for everyone.

'Ryan Giggs? Who's that?'

'Oh, Ryan Wilson has changed his name!'

Despite the problems off the pitch, Ryan was playing better than ever on it. Sport was exactly the escape that he needed and he worked really hard to improve every aspect of his game. As he grew stronger and taller, Ryan became even faster too. The defenders in the youth league had no chance.

Eric Harrison loved coaching Ryan. Watching him play every Saturday was the favourite part of his week. Ryan could get the ball anywhere on the pitch, even in his own half, and make something amazing happen. He could score goals and he could make goals – there was nothing that he couldn't do and he made football so entertaining.

'Sometimes I don't know why the other team even turns up!' Adrian Doherty joked.

With Adrian on the right wing and Ryan on the left, it was a ninety-minute nightmare for their opponents. Big defenders would try to kick Ryan but often they couldn't get close enough to make contact.

There was also a quiet determination to Ryan. He didn't say much, but there was a fire in his eyes and a hunger to succeed. He was fully focused on becoming the best. That was the perfect attitude for United and there was a massive buzz throughout the club about 'the new George Best'.

'Wow, that kid's going to be a superstar,' first-team defender Steve Bruce said when he first saw him in training. 'He can run like the wind!'

Manchester United and England legend Sir Bobby Charlton often went down to 'The Cliff' to watch the youth teams. It didn't take him long to notice Ryan.

'Who's that kid?' he asked as the winger made a fool of another defender. 'He's a very special talent!'

The United supporters loved to watch young, local players in their team, and word spread very quickly about Ryan.

'I've never seen so many fans turn up for an Under-18s match!' Eric told Ferguson.

United were desperate for a new left winger and so it wasn't a question of *if* Ryan would join the senior first team. It was just a question of *when*.

Ferguson kept a close eye on Ryan and all of the other youngsters. When United played at home, he would watch the first half of the youth game in the morning and then rush back to Old Trafford. He was delighted with Ryan's progress but the youth was still only sixteen.

'He's a special talent but we don't want to rush him,' Fergie told his coaches. 'I know he is good enough but is he ready for the fame and the media? His potential is incredible but I just want what's best for him.'

Ryan was happy to listen to his manager and

develop at this own speed. On his seventeenth
birthday, he signed his first professional contract with
Manchester United.

'They're paying me £120 a week,' he boasted to his
mates Stuart and Simon. They were both still studying
at college and so that money sounded like a fortune to
them.

'Now I remember why we're friends with you!'
Stuart laughed.

United didn't make Ryan's life easy, however.
The young players had to do lots of boring tasks to
earn their wages. They weren't football stars yet.
Sometimes, Ryan had to collect the cones and bibs
after training but the worst job was cleaning the
changing rooms.

'Those toilets are disgusting!' he complained to
Darren Ferguson. Darren was the manager's son but
he still had to do the horrible chores too. 'I really
thought I was going to be sick.'

The Manchester United players looked so big and
strong and they could be pretty scary sometimes,
but they also gave Ryan lots of good advice. Captain

Bryan Robson often gave him tips about how to handle the pressure.

'When everyone's talking about you, you just have to learn to block out the noise,' he said.

Ryan was grateful that everyone was trying to protect him but it was time to test himself at the highest level.

'I really don't want to lose you from the youth team,' Eric told him, 'but I can't wait to see you playing in front of 60,000 fans at Old Trafford. They need to see just how good you are.'

Ryan nodded and smiled. He was ready to shine in the first team.

CHAPTER 11

FIRST GAME, FIRST GOAL

After many great performances for the reserves, Ryan was finally called up to the first team squad for Manchester United's league trip to Sheffield United. Everyone was really excited for him but he remained cool and calm.

'Do you think you'll get to play?' Rhodri asked him. He couldn't wait to boast to his mates that his brother was a regular starter for United.

'I don't think so,' he replied. 'There are quite a few injuries, so they're just bringing a few of us youngsters along for the experience.'

It was fun to travel on the team coach with stars like Bryan Robson, Steve Bruce, Brian McClair and

Welsh hero Mark Hughes. Ryan was still pretty shy around them but he listened to their conversations and laughed at their jokes. In the end, United lost 2-1 and Ryan didn't even leave the bench, but he knew he was getting closer and closer.

'You'll come on next week, I'm sure of it,' Steve told him as they said goodbye back in Manchester.

Ryan preferred to stay realistic about his chances. That way, he wouldn't be disappointed. At Old Trafford against Everton, he was hoping that he might get ten minutes at the end of the game, so in the first half he was still pretty relaxed on the bench. Even when left-back Denis Irwin was limping off, he didn't expect what happened next.

'Ryan, get ready!' United's assistant manager Archie Knox shouted. 'You're coming on!'

What? Now? There were still sixty minutes of the match to go. Ryan took a deep breath and quickly took off his tracksuit. Wearing the Number 14 shirt, he ran on to the pitch with the sound of 45,000 fans in his ears. There was enough adrenaline running through his body for the whole team to share.

'Ryan's coming on!' Margaret shouted at the TV back in Wales, as TV commentator Martin Tyler introduced him to the world:

What an opportunity this is for Ryan Giggs, the seventeen-year-old!

Ryan played in attack with Danny Wallace and he never stopped running. He didn't quite get the space to work his usual magic but he caused problems for the Everton defence with his speed and energy. Every time he got the ball, there was an excitement in the Old Trafford air. 'The new George Best' was finally in the team – was he really as good as everyone said he was?

In the second half, Ryan got the ball on the left, just outside the penalty area. This was his favourite area, his danger zone. But instead of dribbling, he looked up and whipped a great cross into the box for Danny to run on to. He looked certain to score but at the last moment, he couldn't quite get enough power on his header and it drifted wide.

United lost 2-0 but Ferguson had one major reason to smile.

'Well done today, kid,' he said to Ryan at the final whistle, putting an arm around his shoulder. 'It was a gloomy day in many ways but you were certainly the bright spot!'

The smile didn't leave Ryan's face for days. He had made his United debut and despite all of the pressure, he hadn't let the team down.

'I think you'll play again next week too!' Rhodri said.

Ryan wasn't so sure. Lee Sharpe was only a few years older than him and he was playing very well on the left wing for Manchester United. Lee was now an England international, so Ryan knew it would be very difficult to take his starting spot.

Two months went by and Ryan didn't play again. It was frustrating but he knew that Ferguson liked to introduce his youngsters slowly.

'Lee's in incredible form and I'm only seventeen!' was Ryan's answer if anyone asked him about it but really he was itching to get back out on the pitch.

Two hours before the big Manchester derby against City, the United players were called into the dressing room for the team news. Ferguson stood at

the front with his tactics board and went through
the starting eleven one by one: 'Goalkeeper. . . Gary
Walsh. Right-back. . . Denis Irwin. Right Wing. . .
Brian McClair. Centre Forward. . . Mark Hughes.
Left Wing. . . Ryan Giggs.'

Ryan wasn't really listening and so it was a real
surprise to hear Ferguson call out his name. He
couldn't believe it – not only was he playing but
he was starting the match. He was making his full
United debut in the derby! Suddenly, the nerves took
over and he could feel the sweat dripping down his
forehead.

'Don't worry, you'll be great!' Mark told him.

By the time that the match kicked off, Ryan was
more excited than nervous. With Lee Sharpe not
playing, this was a big opportunity for Ryan to show
Fergie what he could offer. Every time he got the ball,
he looked to dribble forward. He wasn't scared of
being tackled or making mistakes, and the United fans
loved his confidence. He used his pace and trickery
to beat the City right-back again and again. His final
crosses were a bit disappointing but Ryan kept going.

After twenty minutes, Denis played the ball up to Mark, who flicked it cleverly out to Brian on the wing. Ryan sprinted into the penalty area and towards the front post. Brian's cross was deflected into his path and Ryan stuck out his foot but he didn't touch it. Luckily, the goalkeeper missed it and the ball bounced off defender Colin Hendry and into the net.

*Goooooooooooooooooooooaaaaaaaaaaaaaaaaaaaaaaaa
lllllllllllllllllllllllllllllll!!!!!!!!!!!!!*

Ryan's teammates ran over to celebrate with him.

'Was that your goal?' Mark asked.

Ryan didn't know whether to lie or be honest. 'I'm not sure – the ball might have brushed my shoelace!' he said in the end.

Mark laughed. 'The shoelace is enough – we'll call that your goal!'

United won 1-0 and Ryan was the derby hero. It was a day that he would never, ever forget.

'What a performance!' Ferguson said with a big smile on his face. He loved it when his youngsters did him proud. 'This season is nearly over but I have a feeling you're going to be unstoppable next year!'

CHAPTER 12

GROWING UP
IN PUBLIC

With Mark Hughes chasing after him, the Norwich defender tried to pass the ball back to his goalkeeper. But he'd forgotten about the speed of Manchester United's young superstar. Ryan pounced on the mistake and got there first. He calmly dribbled the ball round the keeper and passed it into the net.

Goooooooooooooooooooooooaaaaaaaaaaaaaaaaaaaaa aaaalllllllllllllllllllllllllllllllllll!!!!!

'It's nice to get my first proper United goal!' he joked with Brian.

With a 3-0 win, the Red Devils were flying at the top of the First Division. Ryan was playing far more football than he had expected but he enjoyed every minute of it. He was living the dream and the fans loved him.

Giggsy! Giggsy! Giggsy!

Against West Ham, Brian went on a brilliant run down the right. There were strikers around the six-yard box but he spotted Ryan's late run from the left. Ryan was full of confidence and as the cross came to him, he decided to hit it first time and on the volley. He caught it perfectly and the ball thundered into the bottom corner of the net.

Goooooooooooooooooooooooooooaaaaaaaaaaaaaaa aaaaaaaaalllllllllllllllllll!!!!!!!!

'Wow, what technique!' Ferguson said to himself as he celebrated on the touchline.

He had always known that Ryan would be a star but even he was surprised by the speed of the boy's progress. Ryan looked so comfortable already, like he had been playing professional football for years. But he was still only a teenager and Fergie did as much as he could to protect him from the media spotlight.

'Is Giggs available to speak to us?' the reporters asked him every week.

Ferguson stood strong. 'No, I'm afraid he won't be doing interviews at this stage of his career.'

In just six months, Ryan's whole life changed. Suddenly, there were crowds of people watching him at training and following him everywhere he went. Everyone wanted to talk to him, have pictures with him, and get his autograph. It was exhausting.

Ryan, we love you!

With his good looks and long, curly hair, the girls loved him and screamed when he walked past. His face was everywhere: on the TV, on the back page of all the newspapers, on the adverts in magazines.

'Here comes the poster boy!' his United teammates teased. Sometimes they put up his model photos in the changing room. Their job was to keep his feet on the ground.

'Bryan, do you think I should ask the boss for a club car?' Ryan asked one day in the changing room after training.

'Yeah, why not?' Bryan replied. 'How many games have you played now?'

'About twenty.'

'Then you deserve one and I'm sure Fergie will agree.'

Thinking that he had his teammate's support, Ryan went up to speak to his manager. As soon as he left the room, the players fell about laughing. They all knew that Giggsy was in for the shock of his life. They crept up the stairs to listen to Fergie's reaction.

'Who do you think you are, kid?' he exploded. 'You're not even a proper player yet – get out!'

When Ryan walked out of Fergie's office, the players were still there laughing. It was one of the best tricks they had ever played.

'That's the last time I listen to you!' he said before storming off.

Ryan wasn't yet an experienced professional but he was soon an international footballer. In October 1991, Wales manager Terry Yorath called him up into the senior squad for their Euro 1992 qualification match against Germany. It was a very proud moment for Ryan and he couldn't wait to tell his family.

'I only started playing for the Under-21s a few months ago!' he said to his grandparents on the phone.

'Yes but it doesn't take a genius to work out that you're ready to play with the big boys,' Dennis replied. He would always be his grandson's biggest fan.

Ryan was nervous about meeting Welsh legends like Ian Rush and Neville Southall but luckily Mark was there from Manchester United, and Leeds United midfielder Gary Speed was a younger, friendly face.

'Welcome to the team!' Gary said, shaking his hand. 'My name's Gary but everyone calls me Speedy. I'll be your roommate and as long as you don't snore, we'll get on really well.'

Ryan watched from the subs bench with Speedy as Germany raced into a 4-0 lead. It was a really bad start to his Welsh career but perhaps he could come on and make a difference? After Wales scored a late penalty, Ryan got his chance. Aged 17 years and 321 days, he was their youngest ever player. There was nothing he could do about the scoreline but he was so happy to be a 'Dragon', representing the country that he loved.

'I really want to play at a major international

tournament,' he told Speedy as they walked off the pitch together. 'It might take a few years but I think me and you can help us get there.'

Everything was happening so quickly for Ryan. Back in England, he tried his best to ignore the fame but he was a young celebrity and the Manchester nightlife was fun. Once, when they should have been resting before a big game, Ryan and Lee decided to have a house party. What Ryan didn't know was that Ferguson had spies all around the city, including Ryan's mum. When she told him, Fergie drove straight to Lee's house.

One of Ryan's friends answered the door but the United manager could see Ryan in the living room, up way beyond the bed-time the players were supposed to keep to, drinking a bottle of beer and talking to girls.

'Right, party's over!' Fergie shouted, storming through the house.

Once everyone else had left, he spoke to his players.

'Look, I know it's tough to grow up in the public eye but this is not acceptable! If you carry on misbehaving, you won't play for United again. Do you understand me? If it's the fast cars and the flashy clothes that you want, then I don't want you at this club. If I catch either of you partying like this again, there will be big trouble!'

Ryan had never seen Fergie look so angry. His face had gone bright red and he looked like he was about to burst. Ryan needed a wake-up call and this was it. He was desperate to become a United legend and he wasn't going to let anything stop him. He knew lots of examples of players with plenty of potential who had wasted their talent.

'I don't want to join that list,' he told himself.

And also, he never wanted to see Fergie look so furious ever again.

From that moment on, Ryan stayed away from the limelight and focused on football. But the expectations were so great that it was impossible for him to live up to them every week. In some games he was magical, and in others he was quiet. He never stopped running but defences now knew about his pace and skill. They watched him closely and double-marked him. And if all else failed, they fouled him.

It was a steep learning curve for a youngster, and Ferguson didn't always make it easy for him. He was a tough manager who expected a lot from his players. And he could be really scary when he wasn't happy. When Fergie got really, really angry, Ryan's teammates called it 'the hairdryer treatment'.

'When he shouts, it feels like really hot air, right in your face,' they explained.

If Ryan had a bad game, the manager always told him:

'What happened today? You barely touched the ball. We don't pay you to stay away from the action!'

Ryan hated 'the hairdryer treatment'. He sat at the back of the team coach on his own and sulked. It was so unfair – he had won the PFA Young Player of the Year award but he wasn't Superman! The senior players left him alone for a bit and then when he'd calmed down, one of them went to speak to him.

'Forget about today,' Steve Bruce said, putting an arm around his shoulder. 'Don't worry, the gaffer isn't annoyed; he's just trying to get the best out of you. Next week, you'll get it right!'

CHAPTER 13

TROPHY TIME

'Ryan, did you hear what George Best said about you?' Margaret asked excitedly on the phone. Before he could answer, she read it out to him. 'He said, "He's got terrific skill and he's going to be a great, great player. They might be saying I'm the second Ryan Giggs if he keeps playing like this." What kind words!'

'Yes, I thanked him the other day,' Ryan replied coolly.

'You met George Best the other day?' Margaret screamed. He was worried that his grandma might faint. 'Why didn't you tell me?!'

'We filmed a TV show together,' he explained. 'We

had a few drinks in the pub and played some pool.
He's a really nice guy.'

Ryan was the hottest player in British football and
Manchester United were the hottest team. They had
finished second in the last season of the First Division
but after a shaky start in the new 'Premier League',
they were unstoppable. In attack, Frenchman Eric
Cantona was a brilliant new signing alongside Brian,
Mark and Ryan. The goals just kept flowing.

Against Tottenham Hotspur, the right-back chested
the ball down but slipped. It was a huge mistake
– Ryan was there in a flash. He won the ball and
immediately nutmegged the centre-back. He ran
towards goal and as the keeper came out to stop him,
he dribbled round him and shot into the net.

*Gooooooooooooooooooooooaaaaaaaaaaaaaaaaaallllll
lllllllllllllllllllllllllllllllllll!!!!!!!!!!!*

By February 1993, United were fighting Aston Villa
and Norwich for the title. Every point was crucial.
Against Southampton, they were running out of time
to score. Eric Cantona got the ball on the left and
looked up; Ryan was the only United player making

a run into the box, and he found him with a perfect pass. The goalkeeper stood up tall and tried to guess where the shot would go. But Ryan wasn't worried; he pretended to hit it to the left but delayed and then hit it to the right instead.

Goooooooooooooooooaaaaaaaaaaaaaaaaaaaaallllllllll llllllllllllllllllllllllll!!!!!!!!!!!!!!!!!

A minute later, Mark's clever header fell to Ryan's feet and he scored a second.

'Your finishing is better than our actual strikers!' Paul Ince joked as they celebrated the important win.

Ryan was scoring lots of goals for United but he still hadn't put the ball in the net for Wales. His country needed him to start scoring soon.

'At this rate, we definitely won't qualify for the 1994 World Cup,' he told his national teammate Gary Speed. 'Romania and Belgium are running away with the group.'

'Don't be so hard on yourself,' Speedy replied. 'You've only played five games for us!'

At home against Belgium, Wales won an early free kick just outside the penalty area. It was perfect for a left-footed, curling strike. With his family watching in the stands, Ryan waited for the referee's whistle. He took a long run-up and hit his shot with lots of power. The ball flew over the wall and into the top corner before the goalkeeper even knew what was going on.

Gooooooooooooooooooooooooooooooaaaaaaaaaaaaaa aaaaalllllllllllllllllllllllllll!!!!!!!!!!

The Welsh fans went crazy. Ryan ran towards the corner flag to celebrate and Speedy gave him a big hug. It was such a relief to finally get his first international goal.

In early May 1993, United were finally crowned Premier League champions. It was a huge relief to win the club's first league title in twenty-six years. The wait was over. There was a big party in Manchester that night, and Ryan and his teammates had the time of their lives.

The next day, however, they had another match to play, against Blackburn Rovers. As the team walked out on to the pitch, the crowd stood to applaud and cheer their heroes. The atmosphere was incredible.

It was an amazing moment for the players and Ryan walked around the pitch, clapping back. The team couldn't have done it without the amazing Old Trafford support.

Giggsy! Giggsy! Giggsy!

United started slowly after their big night of celebrations. They were 1-0 down but they couldn't let their fans down. After twenty minutes, they won a free kick about thirty yards from goal.

'I've got this,' Ryan told his teammates. He was full of confidence.

'Are you sure?' Lee asked. 'The goal is a long way away!'

Ryan didn't listen. When the referee blew his whistle, he curled the ball straight into the top left corner.

Goooooooooooooooooooaaaaaaaaaaaaaaaaaaalllllllllllll lllllllllllllllll!!!!!!!!!!!!!!!!!!

Ryan ran and jumped into Eric's arms. There was no better way to end an amazing season.

'What were you saying to me back there?' Ryan asked Lee as they ran back for the restart.

Lee laughed. 'I take it all back – what a strike! I didn't know you could hit the ball that hard.'

United won the match and afterwards, the captains Steve and Bryan lifted the beautiful silver and gold trophy together in front of the 40,000 fans. Ryan would never forget that night, even though there were many more successful nights to come.

'Right, it's time to get our jackets on!' Incey laughed as they got back into the changing room. Ryan and Paul had decided to challenge each other – who could wear the loudest jacket for the trophy photos? Incey went for black and white tartan, and Ryan wore a black and white, zebra-print jacket with a tie covered in big, colourful spots.

'I've definitely won this!' Ryan cheered and everyone agreed. He looked awful!

With such talented players and a great team spirit, United were determined to keep winning. They set themselves new targets for the 1993–94 season.

'I want to win the league again and at least one cup,' Ryan told Lee in preseason training. 'And I want to score even more goals than last year!'

Ryan scored in their first Premiership match against Norwich and never looked back. He scored free kicks, volleys, tap-ins, even headers. He was Britain's biggest superstar and the commentators loved him:

As they say in Wales, that's Ryan Giggs for you!

Away at Liverpool, Ryan won the ball and galloped forward. As the defenders closed in for the tackle, he spotted that the goalkeeper was off his line. Ryan decided that it was worth a try; he chipped the ball towards the right-hand corner. The keeper stretched his arm as high as it would go but he couldn't reach it.

Goooooooooooooooooooooooaaaaaaaaaaaaaaaaalllll lllllllllllllllllllllllll!!!!!!!!!!!!!!!!

Incey ran across the pitch and jumped on his back. They had their own special goal celebration to do, which they had practised in training.

But Ryan's favourite goals were the ones where he dribbled round lots of players. Against QPR, he swerved right to beat the first defender, then left to beat the next two, before shooting into the net. His balance and control allowed him to change direction so quickly. He was like the Pied Piper of Hamelin, leading his opponents on a merry dance.

'Do you even sweat?' Lee asked. 'I've never seen you look tired at all!'

By the end of that 1993–94 season, Manchester United had won the League and FA Cup double, just as Ryan had hoped. As an individual, he was also named the PFA Young Player of the Year for a second time in three years. Meanwhile, rising in the ranks at United were the promising likes of midfielders Nicky Butt, Paul Scholes and David Beckham.

'I don't really think of myself as a youngster anymore,' he told his mum after the awards ceremony. 'Compared to Scholesy and Becks, I'm an old man!'

CHAPTER 14

CLASS OF '92

'Ferguson needs to buy players,' former Liverpool
player Alan Hansen told the British public on *Match
of the Day*. 'You can't win anything with kids.'

After losing the Premier League title to Blackburn,
the United manager sold Mark, Incey and Andrei
Kanchelskis. But in the first game of the 1995–96
season, his new team had just lost 3-1 to Aston Villa.
Rather than spending lots of money, Fergie decided to
trust his latest crop of youngsters: not only Ryan but also
defenders Gary and Phil Neville, midfielders Paul Scholes
and Nicky Butt, and on the right wing, David Beckham.

'We'll see about that!' was the team's response to
Hansen's prediction.

A few years earlier, 'The Class of '92' had taken the FA Youth Cup by storm. Ryan was a couple of years older than the others but he still played with them and they were all best mates. Apart from David Beckham, they had all grown up in the Manchester area.

'How are you finding life up North, Becks?' they liked to joke. David was from London. 'Is it too cold and wet?'

Ryan was their leader. He was playing really well for the United first team and that was a great inspiration for the others.

'Hopefully we'll all be joining you there soon!' Gary said.

In the first leg of the 1992 final against Crystal Palace, Nicky Butt scored two goals and Becks scored the other in a 3-1 victory. For the second leg at Old Trafford, over 15,000 fans turned up to watch. Word was spreading quickly about the talented United youth team. When Nicky nearly scored with an acrobatic overhead kick, the supporters cheered loudly. It was great to see them having fun.

'If that had gone in, it would have been the best goal ever!' he told Ryan.

'Yes and you would never have stopped talking about it!' he replied with a smile.

Ryan's perfect cross from the left set up United's third goal to make it 3-2 on the night, and 6-3 on aggregate. As captain, Ryan lifted the trophy but Becks, Nicky and Gary were right behind him. It was a great moment for a group of kids with a bright future ahead of them.

'This is the best youth team I've ever coached,' Eric Harrison told the media.

The next year, it got even better when Scholesy and Phil Neville joined them. But in the final against Leeds, they lost 4-1 on aggregate. Scholesy scored a penalty but both matches were a disaster.

'It's because you didn't have me!' Ryan said when it was safe to make a joke. He had stopped playing youth football because he was playing in the Premier League every week.

By the end of the 1994–95 season, all six of that 'Class of '92' had made their first team debuts. In an FA Cup match against Wrexham, they showed exactly what they could do together. Scholesy passed the ball to Phil on the left, who passed it back and kept running into the box. Scholesy's one-two was perfect and Phil looked up to see who was waiting for the cross. Ryan made a run at the back post and slotted the ball past the keeper.

Goooooooooooooooooooooaaaaaaaaaaaaaaaaaaaalll lllllllllllllllllllllllll!!!!!!!!!!!!!!!

Ryan ran to celebrate with Phil. 'What a move!'

The 'Class of '92' were excited about the year ahead. They were determined to become Premier League regulars and win lots of trophies.

'We're ready to take over this team!' Becks said with lots of confidence. 'It's our time now!'

* * *

Undeterred after their defeat against Aston Villa at the start of the 1995–96 season, United recovered and grew stronger and stronger. The 'Class of '92' were soon unstoppable. Ryan loved playing with his mates and it made him better than ever.

Against Everton, Becks ran at the defence and at just the right moment, he passed it across to Ryan. Ryan placed his shot in the bottom corner. They made it look so easy. And whenever he didn't score, then Scholesy or Becks scored instead. Opponents couldn't cope with their energy, skill and teamwork.

'Do you remember what Alan Hansen said?' Ryan laughed with the others. 'We've got seven games left and we're top of the league. We're going to win this!'

In the Manchester derby, United were heading for a 2-2 draw. One point wouldn't be enough to keep them above Kevin Keegan's Newcastle United team in the table. Eric ran forward with the ball and slipped it to Ryan on the left. He was in great goalscoring form and he knew that the defender would expect him to dribble. So Ryan hit the shot straight away, as hard as he could. The goalkeeper dived towards the top left corner but he couldn't keep it out.

Goooooooooooooooooaaaaaaaaaaaaaaaaaaaaaalllllllll lllllllllllllllllllll!!!!!!!!!!!!!!!!

What a moment to score! Ryan ran towards the United fans with one arm up in the air. His teammates chased after him.

'You love scoring against City, don't you!' Lee shouted.

In their final game of the season against Middlesbrough, United only needed one point to win the Premiership. But the 'Class of '92' didn't believe in draws. Ryan swung a corner to the back post and centre-back David May jumped high and headed into the net.

They were winning now – would they sit back and defend? No, that wasn't the United way. From another Ryan corner, Andy Cole made it 2-0. Still, they continued to attack. Nicky passed to Ryan and he ran towards goal. The defenders backed away in fear. As he got near the penalty area, he decided to shoot. The ball flew like an arrow into the back of the net.

*Goooooooooooooaaaaaaaaaaaaaaaaaaaaaallllllllllll
llllllllllllllllll!!!!!!!!!!!!!!!!!*

Everything Ryan touched seemed to turn to gold.
It was a very entertaining end to a very entertaining
season. On the touchline, Fergie couldn't stop
smiling. He looked at his watch and waited for the
final whistle.

The 'Class of '92' jumped up and down together
– they had achieved the impossible! It was beyond
Ryan's wildest dreams. They ran to thank their
manager.

'I feel like a very proud father!' Fergie said as his
youngsters hugged him. 'I believed in you guys – and
boy, did you repay my faith!'

CHAPTER 15

THE TREBLE PART I – PREMIER LEAGUE

'I know all about Dwight Yorke but what about Jaap Stam and Jesper Blomqvist?' Ryan asked as the squad got ready for the 1998–99 season. After losing the title to Arsenal, Ferguson had made some expensive new signings.

'Jaap is a centre-back – they call him "The Rock" in Holland,' Gary Neville replied. If he wasn't playing football, he was always watching it. He knew everything. 'And Jesper is a left winger, so you better watch out, Giggsy!'

Ryan wasn't too worried about having competition but he was desperate to get back to his best. At twenty-five, he was meant to be at his peak but a hamstring injury had kept him out at the end of the previous season, just when his team needed him the most.

'Hopefully we won't need him but he'll warm the bench up nicely!' Ryan joked.

With United competing for lots of trophies at the same time, it was important to have a really good squad. If Ryan, Scholesy, Roy Keane or Becks couldn't play, they had good midfield replacements like Nicky and Jesper. And in attack, there was no doubt that Teddy Sheringham, Ole Gunnar Solskjær, Andy Cole and Dwight Yorke would score lots and lots of goals between them.

But United started badly in the Premier League. They drew their first two games but, after winning the next two, then lost 3-0 to rivals Arsenal.

'That was just not good enough today!' Ferguson shouted angrily in the dressing room afterwards. 'If we keep playing like that, we'll be lucky to avoid relegation!'

With the manager's words in their ears, United got back to their winning ways. The team was playing well but Ryan certainly wasn't scoring as often as he used to.

'Don't worry about goals,' Fergie told him. 'As long as you're still terrorising defences and creating chances, that's all we care about! We've got more strikers than ever to put the ball in the net.'

Against Nottingham Forest, Teddy passed to Becks, who spotted Ryan's forward run. As he dribbled into the penalty area, the goalkeeper dived to make a save. Ryan coolly chipped the ball over him and into the net.

Goooooooooooooooooooooaaaaaaaaaaaaaaaaaallllllllllll llllllllllllllllllllllllll!!!!!!!!!!!!!!!!!

Ryan jumped into the air and pumped his fist. It was good to be back on the scoresheet.

'That's the Giggsy we know and love!' Nicky shouted, giving him a big hug.

By the end of January, United were top of the table but Arsenal were right behind them. The Red Devils couldn't afford to make any mistakes. But, a few weeks after that, away at Coventry City, they were drawing 0-0, with about ten minutes to go.

'Come on, we've got to win this!' Keano shouted at his teammates.

Ryan ran forward and passed to Becks out on the right wing. They had a plan. Ole would run towards the front post for the cross, so Ryan made his classic run towards the back post. He got there just in time to volley the ball past the goalkeeper. It wasn't his best strike but the defender on the line couldn't stop it from going in.

Goooooooooooooooooooaaaaaaaaaaaaaaaaaallllllllllll lllllllllllllllllllllllll!!!!!!!!!!!!!!!

'I had a feeling that you'd rescue us today!' Scholesy said as they celebrated.

Ryan loved being the matchwinner. Some players panicked when the pressure was on but he loved it. This was why he had become a professional footballer – to play at the top level in the biggest matches.

By late April, with three games of the season to go, United had slipped back to second place, three points behind the Gunners.

'We know what we have to do,' Ryan said calmly.

He already had lots of experience of the race for the title. 'We just have to get all nine points!'

Dwight scored the winner in the first match against Middlesbrough.

'Right, two more victories and we'll be champions again!' Keano told them after the game. They had to stay focused right until the end.

Though Arsenal lost to Leeds, Manchester United could only draw with Blackburn – with one match left, they were one point ahead. It was going to be a very exciting final day.

'Arsenal will definitely beat Aston Villa at home,' Ryan discussed with his teammates before kick-off. He couldn't wait for the game to start. 'So we have to beat Tottenham. If we lose or draw, it's over!'

Early on, Ryan crossed from the left and Dwight shot towards goal... but the keeper saved it. Then from a Becks corner, Ryan jumped high for the header but again, the keeper saved it.

'Keep going, we'll get the goal eventually!' Gary cheered from defence.

But out of nowhere, Tottenham took the lead. For

a second, the United players stood there in shock. Suddenly, they needed not one but two goals.

'Come on, we can do this!' Keano shouted.

United had chance after chance but they just couldn't get the ball in the net. Everyone was starting to get nervous.

'We're rushing things!' Ryan said. 'We need to stay calm and play like we normally do.'

Just before half-time, Scholesy won the ball and passed to Ryan. He dribbled forward and then passed back to Scholesy. They were being patient. Scholesy looked up and saw Becks making a great run into the box. Becks took one touch and blasted his shot into the top corner. 1-1!

'Game on!' he shouted as Old Trafford went wild.

Ferguson brought on Andy for Teddy, and three minutes later, he got his opportunity. Gary played a beautiful pass over the top of the defence and Andy was in lots of space. He controlled the ball brilliantly and as the keeper rushed out to block him, he side-footed it over his head. 2-1!

Apart from the goalkeeper, the whole team

jumped on Andy. The atmosphere in the stadium was incredible. United just needed to hold on for another forty-five minutes.

When the final whistle went, the players jumped for joy. Against a very good Arsenal team, they had won another Premier League title. Ferguson walked around the pitch, smiling and clapping to the fans. Half an hour later, Keano lifted the trophy high high above his head.

Campeones, Campeones, Olé Olé Olé!

It was another unbelievable day for Ryan but the season wasn't over. They still had two more finals to play – the FA Cup and then the Champions League.

'One down, two to go!' Ryan said happily.

CHAPTER 16

THE TREBLE PART II = THE FA CUP

Ryan had already won the FA Cup twice in his career but that didn't mean he was any less determined to win it again.

'In 1994, Eric was the star man and he was the star in 1996 too!' he told Becks. 'We need to win the FA Cup with this new team and I want to be a hero this time.'

In the third round, United were beating Middlesbrough 2-1 with only a minute to go. It would be good to get another goal to make sure of the victory. Ryan was the man for the job. He dribbled in from the left, looking for his opportunity to break through the defence. Ole called for the ball with his back to goal. Ryan passed to him and then kept running into the box for a brilliant one-two. He was far too quick for the Middlesbrough defenders and he slotted the ball under the keeper.

Goooooooooooooooooooooooaaaaaaaaaaaaaaaaaaaaaa alllllllllllllllllllll!!!!!!!!!!!

'Now we're definitely through to the next round!' Dwight said, lifting Ryan into the air.

United weren't always at their best but their desire to win took them all the way to the semi-finals. Their opponents were league rivals, Arsenal.

'Whoever wins this semi will win the cup,' Gary predicted. 'Let's make sure that it's us!'

But at Villa Park neither team could score, even after 120 minutes of football, including extra time. There would have to be a replay.

'I can't believe they disallowed that goal!' Ryan moaned as they walked off the pitch. He was really frustrated because Keano had scored from his brilliant cross but the referee claimed it was offside.

'Yeah, what a rubbish decision!' Keano replied. 'The last thing we need at the moment is another game to play.'

In the final month of the season, United were still challenging for the FA Cup, the Premier League *and* the Champions League. The chance to win the Treble was too good to miss but it was exhausting for the players. They weren't superheroes; sometimes they needed to rest so that they didn't get injured.

'I'm sorry, we need to keep you fit for the Champions League semi-final against Juventus,' Ferguson told Ryan before the FA Cup replay. 'But you'll be a substitute in case we need your magic!'

Ryan always hated missing a match but he understood his manager's choice. He cheered from the bench as United took the lead thanks to a wonder goal from Becks. They were playing well but they couldn't score a second time. After sixty minutes, Ryan got the call that he was waiting for.

'Giggsy, we need that magic!' United's assistant manager, Steve McClaren, shouted to him.

But a few minutes after he came on, Dennis Bergkamp scored to make it 1-1 and with fifteen minutes to go, Keano was sent off. It was turning into a nightmare and Ryan was struggling to help his team.

He kept giving the ball away when they were trying to hold on and take the game to penalties.

'Giggsy, we've only got ten men!' Gary reminded him. 'We don't have the energy to attack, so we have to keep it simple.'

In the second-half of extra time, Patrick Vieira's pass fell to Ryan just inside his own half. There was lots of space to attack and there were tired defenders everywhere.

'Dribble towards the corner flag!' Fergie shouted on the touchline. 'Just waste some time – we're nearly there.'

But Ryan didn't listen; he had a better idea. He did what was natural to him; he ran forward, and the Arsenal defenders backed away. They knew what Ryan could do and they were scared. He dribbled past Vieira, and then past Lee Dixon. On the edge of the penalty area, there were two Arsenal players in front of him. The safe option was to pass but Ryan wanted to be the hero and he knew that he had the skill to do it. With two brilliant touches, he dribbled between the defenders!

Giggsy! Giggsy! Giggsy!

The United fans were on their feet cheering, and the players just stood and watched their wing wizard racing towards goal. Surely he couldn't score the winner?

As a defender flew in for the tackle, Ryan knew it was time to shoot. He was quite wide on the left but he had scored many goals from that angle. Just like he used to on the fields of Pentrebane, Ryan hit the shot as hard as he could. The ball rocketed over the Arsenal keeper David Seaman and into the top of the net.

Goooooooooooooooooooooaaaaaaaaaaaaaaaaaaaalll llllllllllllllllllllllllllllllllll!!!!!!!!!

Ryan was normally very calm when he scored but this was no ordinary goal. He would never score another goal as good as this one. Like the fans around him in the stadium, Ryan went wild. He took his shirt off and swung it around his head. His teammates ran after him but it was difficult to keep up with him.

'Giggsy, you're a genius!' Phil shouted. 'That's the best goal I've ever seen.'

Some of the United fans ran on to the pitch to thank their hero. No-one would ever forget United's greatest ever goal. Against the odds, the Red Devils were through to the FA Cup Final and it was all thanks to Ryan.

'You'll never need to buy another drink in Manchester!' Becks joked as they celebrated.

Ryan couldn't believe the reaction in the newspapers the next day. It was the only thing that anyone was talking about. Argentina legend Diego Maradona had scored one of the best goals of all time against England but he said he wished that he had scored that goal against Arsenal. It was a very proud day for all of the Giggs family.

'I really didn't think that life could get any better!' he told his grandparents on the phone.

In the final against Newcastle, Ryan didn't need to do anything as special. After winning 2-0, the players linked arms and jumped up and down together. It was another incredible day at Wembley for Manchester United and the team spirit was clear for all to see. Together, they had won the league and cup double but they had one last challenge left and it was the biggest challenge of them all: the Champions League Final.

'Two down, one to go!' Ryan said happily.

CHAPTER 17

THE TREBLE PART III – THE CHAMPIONS LEAGUE

The UEFA Champions League was the biggest trophy in club football and Ryan was desperate to add a winner's medal to his ever-growing collection. He loved playing against the best teams in Europe but he wouldn't be satisfied until Manchester United were crowned champions for the first time since 1968.

'It's the only medal that I don't have yet!' he discussed with Scholesy ahead of the 1998–99 season. 'We made it to the semi-finals in 1997 and the quarter-finals last year. But I really think our current squad is good enough to go all the way.'

When the groups were announced, the task suddenly got a lot harder. United would be up against

Spanish champions Barcelona and German giants Bayern Munich. Only two of the three teams could qualify for the next stage.

'That's a Group of Death!' Dwight complained but everyone was excited about the challenge. It would be an amazing experience to play at famous stadiums like the Nou Camp and the Olympic Stadium.

'We have to start well,' Ryan told his teammates. 'There's no space for us to slip up.'

At home against Barcelona, Becks attacked down the right wing. He beat the left-back and crossed the ball into the box. It flew over the heads of Dwight and Ole but yet again, Ryan was running in at the back post. He jumped higher than the right-back and powered his header past the goalkeeper.

Goooooooooooooooooooooooaaaaaaaaaaaaaaaaaaaa aalllllllllllllllllllllllllll!!!!!!!!!!!

'I didn't know you could jump that high!' Becks joked as they celebrated.

'Hey, I've scored way more headers than you,' Ryan replied with a smile. 'You're too scared of messing up that beautiful hair!'

In the end, the match finished as a draw and
so did the other three matches against Barcelona
and Bayern Munich. Fortunately, United won both
matches against the other team in the group,
Danish champions Brondby, and so finished in
second place.

'That was tough!' Scholesy said. 'Let's hope we get
an easier opponent in the quarter-finals.'

But Inter Milan were not easy opponents at all.
They had an incredible strikeforce including the
Italian Roberto Baggio, the Brazilian Ronaldo and the
Chilean Iván Zamorano.

'I hope our defence is ready for this,' Nicky said
before kick-off.

'Of course we are!' Gary replied. The confidence
was high in the Old Trafford dressing room. 'Inter will
be lucky if they get a single shot on goal.'

They won 3-1 on aggregate to set up a semi-final
against Italian champions, Juventus. It was yet another
difficult draw for United.

'We're certainly playing against the best around,'
Keano laughed. 'In the last round, we played against

Ronaldo and Baggio. This time, it's Zinedine Zidane and Alessandro Del Piero – bring it on!'

At Old Trafford in the first leg, United were 1-0 down with seconds to go. A home defeat would be a complete disaster. On the right, Becks kicked a hopeful ball back over his head and the goalkeeper could only punch it up in the air. It was chaos in the penalty area but the ball eventually bounced down in front of Ryan. It needed to be a calm finish and he was certainly the right man for the job. Ryan smashed his shot into the top of the net.

Goooooooooooooooooooooaaaaaaaaaaaaaaaaaaaaalllll llllllllllllllllllllllllllllll!!!!!!!!!!!!

The crowd went wild and the players jumped on Ryan.

'Giggsy to the rescue yet again!' Fergie cheered at the final whistle. 'We're still in this, boys!'

United had to win away in Italy, which would be very difficult. It became even more difficult when Ryan injured his ankle after scoring that amazing goal against Arsenal in the FA Cup semi-final.

'Are you sure I can't play?' he asked the club

physio. He was in a lot of pain but it was the worst possible time to get hurt. 'Maybe I could be a substitute?'

'If you play, there's a good chance that you'll miss the FA Cup Final, the rest of the Premier League season, and the Champions League final if we get there.'

No, Ryan couldn't miss all of those important games. 'Okay, I'll have to rest then.'

He hated watching any United game from the sidelines but the second leg against Juventus was really horrible. When the Italian team took a 2-0 lead, Ryan wanted to put his boots on and run out on to the pitch. He needed to help his team.

But in the end, United did the job without him. Keano got the first goal and Dwight got the second. By half-time, the game was tied but that wouldn't be enough.

'Come on, boys!' Ryan shouted as time ran out in the second half.

With less than ten minutes to go, Peter Schmeichel took a long goal kick. The Juventus defender cleared it straight to Dwight, who ran forward and beat two defenders.

'Yes! Yes!' Ryan cheered as he rose to his feet.

As Dwight went round the goalkeeper, he was fouled. Penalty? No, Andy sprinted towards the ball and put it in the net. 3-2 and United were in the Champions League final.

'What a comeback, lads!' Ryan shouted as he joined his teammates in the dressing room. 'We never give up, do we?!'

The only bad news was that Keano and Scholesy were both suspended for the final.

'What a stupid rule!' Ryan said. 'What are we going to do without you?' They were all really good mates who worked together as a team. Everyone had an important role to play.

'The pressure is now on you and Becks to create something special,' Scholesy replied. 'Don't let us down!'

In the final, Bayern Munich were United's opponents again. The atmosphere at the Nou Camp in Barcelona was incredible. 90,000 fans were there to watch the biggest match of the year. As he walked out on to the pitch, Ryan took a deep breath. He had made it to the very top of world football.

Becks moved to the centre with Nicky, Ryan switched to the right wing and Jesper played on the left. It wasn't their best midfield but they were ready to do their best to bring the European trophy back to Manchester.

After five minutes, Bayern won a free-kick and Mario Basler's shot was deflected past Peter. It was the worst possible start for United.

'Keep going!' Ryan shouted. Without Keano and Scholesy, he was one of the senior players now. Some of the players looked upset but there was plenty of time left. 'We've still got about ninety minutes to equalise!'

Ryan did his best in his new role on the right wing. He was always a threat but time was running out.

'Come on, Ryan!' Margaret and Dennis screamed at the TV. The tension was unbearable.

Three added minutes. Can United score? They always score!

Even Peter came up for the corner – it was now or never. Becks's cross was cleared to Ryan on the edge of the penalty area. He didn't have long to react. He volleyed the ball towards goal with his right foot. He didn't strike it very well but it looked like it was heading for the bottom corner. Teddy stuck out a boot to make sure. 1-1!

The noise was incredible as they celebrated the goal. The fans had never stopped believing and neither had the players.

'We can win this now!' Ryan shouted to his teammates.

The Bayern players were in shock and suddenly United were the favourites. From another Becks corner, Teddy headed the ball across and Ole poked it into the net. 2-1!

It was the most amazing end to a Champions League final ever. In less than three minutes, they had gone from losing to winning. It really was the perfect end to a perfect season. Manchester United had won the Treble, the most successful season in the history of the football club.

'We did it!' Ryan shouted as he walked around the pitch with the huge trophy in his hands. He had his boots tied around his neck and a United scarf too. The players stayed on the pitch for hours to share the special moment with the fans. Each player got their turn to lift the trophy and the fans never stopped cheering.

Campeones, Campeones, Olé Olé Olé!

It was hard to believe that it wasn't all a dream. Ryan was a champion of England and now a champion of Europe too.

CHAPTER 18

TIME FOR A CHANGE?

'Giggsy, is it true that you're thinking about going to Italy?' Scholesy asked with a very worried look on his face. He didn't want the gang to break up but it looked like Becks was leaving United – and maybe even Ryan too, as Inter Milan had been trying to sign him for a long time.

'I don't know,' Ryan replied honestly. It was the most difficult decision of his life.

After more than ten years at Old Trafford, things weren't going so well. United won three more Premier League titles after the amazing Treble but by 2003, Ryan was struggling. He always set very high standards for himself and he tried hard to get back to

122

his magical best. But for the first time in his career, he lacked the incredible pace to dribble past every defender in sight.

'Do you think I will get my speed back?' Ryan asked the club physio.

'I don't want to lie to you,' the physio replied. 'It's unlikely after so many hamstring injuries.'

That was terrible news. How could Ryan continue to be a wing wizard without his key weapon? He couldn't stop thinking about it and it affected his performances on the pitch. Against Blackburn in the 2003 League Cup, he could hear the United fans booing him.

'I can't believe it!' Ryan said to Becks. He was really upset. 'After all that I've done for the club in the last decade, how can they turn against me now?'

Against Arsenal in the FA Cup, Ryan made a trademark run down the left and Becks played the perfect pass. Ryan dribbled towards the goal. Surely he would score just like he had against Arsenal in 1999? The Old Trafford crowd held their breath. He took it past the goalkeeper and then past the defender. There was an open goal in front of him but instead of his usual calm finish, Ryan smashed his shot over the bar. He covered his face with his hands – he had never missed such an easy chance.

'Don't worry, we all make mistakes,' Gary told him but it didn't make Ryan feel any better.

'A year ago, there's no way that I would have missed that!'

Ryan told the media that he wasn't finished at United but in private, he wasn't so sure. Fergie had signed the South Americans Juan Sebastián Verón and Diego Forlán, and Ryan's starting spot was in danger. He loved the club but he didn't want to be a substitute.

'Maybe I need a change,' Ryan told his manager. 'This is the only team I've ever played for but I'm not the same player that I used to be.'

Fergie disagreed with his suggestion. 'No, you're going to end your career here at Old Trafford. The problem at the moment is that you think that your talent is all about your speed, but it's not. You're not as quick as you used to be but your football brain is better than ever. You just need to adapt the way that you play. Think more, and dribble less. You're not going anywhere!'

It felt good to have the boss's support and Ryan knew that he was right. He could still be a world-class player but he just needed to be clever and have faith in his other skills.

Against Juventus in the Champions League, Ryan started on the bench but Diego got injured after only five minutes. As Ryan ran on to the field, he knew that it was a huge moment for him. It was time to prove his critics wrong on the biggest stage of all. He was ready to shine.

Ten minutes later, Juan won the ball on the right side of the penalty area and passed to Ryan. This time, Ryan wasn't going to hurry and miss. He controlled the ball and steadied himself, before shooting past the goalkeeper.

Gooooooooooooooooooooaaaaaaaaaaaaaaaaaaaallllllll lllllllllllllllllllllllllll!!!!!!!!!!!

'That's more like it!' Phil shouted as he gave Ryan a big hug.

It was a huge relief to score for his team against such top opponents. He was full of confidence again and just before half-time, he ran at the Juventus defence. He turned inside past the first defender and then past another. He was flying like the old days! They expected him to cut back on to his left foot but Ryan shot with his right foot instead. The ball rolled perfectly into the bottom corner.

What a goal! It was one of the best Ryan had ever scored. He ran towards the United fans and pointed at the back of his shirt – '11 GIGGS'. He was reminding them that he was still a superstar.

'Giggsy, it's great to have you back!' Becks cheered, jumping into his arms.

It was great to *be* back. Manchester United was the only club that he would ever love. He couldn't wait to help them win more trophies.

'Inter will definitely want you after that!' Scholesy joked.

Ryan laughed. 'Shut up, I'm not going anywhere!'

CHAPTER 19

NINE-TIME CHAMPION

'How do you look so fresh?' Gary asked at training the day after a match. 'I'm two years younger than you and I wake up every morning with so many aches and pains. I can barely get out of bed!'

Ryan's answer was one word. 'Yoga.'

Doing lots of stretching every day was really helping to keep his body healthy. By exercising his lower back, his hamstrings had stopped hurting. He felt like a much younger man and it was all thanks to yoga.

'As you get older, you've got to look after yourself more,' Ryan told Gary. 'I want to play until I'm forty!'

He was certainly heading in the right direction. Ryan was thirty-three and he was still a key part of the

United team. Gary was the captain because he loved to shout and organise the team, and Ryan was vice-captain. Everyone looked up to him, especially the new generation of young stars like Cristiano Ronaldo and Wayne Rooney.

'You're a senior player now,' Fergie told him. 'Part of your job is to look after the youngsters.'

Even though Ryan still felt like a teenager, he listened to his manager. He gave them advice about growing up in the spotlight and staying focused on football. He had lots to teach them about being professional. He also led by example on the pitch. He never stopped working hard for the team, closing down defenders and making tackles.

'How many league titles have you won?' he liked to ask them if they were getting too big for their boots. 'I've won eight!'

Ryan was very proud of his record but United had not won the league for three years. He was determined to help his team to beat their rivals Arsenal and Chelsea and become the champions of England again.

'Our team has changed a lot in the last few seasons,' he told Gary in August 2006. Becks, Keano, Phil and Nicky had all left the club, and so had Dwight, Andy and Jaap. 'But I think we're ready to really challenge for the title again!'

Ryan's role in the side was changing too. He was no longer a young, pacy winger; instead, he often played in a more central midfield position, using his vision and experience to create goals for Wayne Rooney, Cristiano Ronaldo and Louis Saha.

'Giggsy, are you trying to steal my position?' Scholesy joked as he set up another goal with a clever through-ball. 'I'm the playmaker around here!'

Ryan still scored important goals too. In his 600th starting appearance for United against Watford, the score was 1-1. When a midfielder made a weak backpass, Ryan was the first to react. He was one on one with the keeper, his favourite battle. He skipped past him in a flash and smashed the ball into the net.

Gooooooooooooooooooooaaaaaaaaaaaaaaaaaaaaaallll lllllllllllllllllllll!!!!!!!!!!!!!!!

Ryan raised his arms to the crowd, showing off his

captain's armband. When United needed him most, he was always there to be the hero.

Ferguson used Ryan carefully and saved him for the big games, especially in Europe. At French club Lille in the second round of the Champions League, United won a free kick in shooting range. The score was 0-0 and an away goal could be vital.

Wayne placed the ball as Lille organised their defensive wall. As they waited, Ryan spotted an opportunity. He curled his shot into the top right corner. The French team were furious but his quick-thinking had won the game for United.

With Cristiano and Wayne scoring the goals and Ryan and Scholesy creating them, they were running away with the Premier League.

'We've been top of the table since October!' Wayne boasted.

But away at Everton in late April 2007, United found themselves losing 2-0.

'Come on boys – this isn't good enough!' Ryan shouted at his players. 'Chelsea are only three points behind us.'

The comeback started from Ryan's corner. The goalkeeper dropped the ball and John O'Shea scored. Cristiano got the second and Wayne got the third. Ryan jumped up onto Wayne's back and shouted up at the celebrating United fans.

'We won't stop until we are Premier League champions!'

After their final home match of the 2006–07 season, the title celebrations began. As the players came back on to the pitch, Old Trafford roared. 'We've Got Our Trophy Back' was written on banners all across the stadium. Ryan and Gary lifted the trophy together, just like Bryan and Steve had fourteen years earlier. Fireworks flew up into the sky.

It was an incredible moment to share with his friends and family. Ryan's children Zachary and Liberty came on to the pitch with him and posed for photos with the trophy.

'This is why we keep playing!' he said to Scholesy and Gary. 'I love days like this and I never want them to end.'

In the dressing room, the players sprayed

champagne and jumped up and down. The party
would go on all night long.

Campeones, Campeones, Olé Olé Olé!

Suddenly, they started singing a different song.
They loved their leader:

He's won it nine times, He's won it nine times,
That boy Giggsy, he's won it nine times!

Ryan was standing towards the back with his medal
around his neck but they pushed him forward into the
middle and poured champagne over his head. As he
wiped his face with his shirt, Ryan had a big grin on
his face.

He'll win it ten times, he'll win it ten times,
That boy Giggsy, he'll win it ten times!

CHAPTER 20

ANOTHER DOUBLE

Cristiano cut in from the left wing and took a shot at goal. It swerved through the air and the Derby goalkeeper could only push it out. Ryan was in the right place to tap it into the net.

Gooooooooooooooooooaaaaaaaaaaaaaaaaaalllllllllllllllll llllllllllllll!!!!!!!!!!!!!!!!!!!!!

It was far from his best goal ever but it was a very important one.

'A hundred league goals – congratulations!' Wayne shouted as Ryan ran to the fans to celebrate. 'It's only taken you seventeen years!'

'Hey, I'm not a striker like you,' he argued. 'A hundred goals is pretty good for a winger!'

A couple of months later, Ryan reached another century. When United played Lyon in the Champions League second round, it was his hundredth appearance in the tournament.

'Wow, I feel so old!' he laughed. He could still remember his first appearance against Hungarian team Kispest Honvéd, way back in 1993.

'You may be old but you're still amazing!' Cristiano replied.

In order to stay fit, Ryan had made the very difficult decision to retire from international football. Over sixteen years, he had played sixty-four matches for Wales and scored twelve goals. He had achieved his dream of captaining his country but they had failed to qualify for a World Cup or European Championships. That was very disappointing but Ryan had done his best.

'We got so close to playing at Euro 2004,' Ryan reminded Gary Speed when they talked about his announcement. Losing by a single goal to Russia in the play-offs had been one of the most heartbreaking moments of his career. 'But it's the right time for me

MATT AND TOM OLDFIELD

to move on and let the next generation take over. I just can't play as much football as I used to.'

It was very good news for United. Ryan was a key player as they chased another Premier League and Champions League double. Ryan never got tired of competing for trophies.

'When I stop feeling excited, I'll give up,' he told Gary.

'You'll be playing until you're sixty then!' Gary replied.

The race for the 2007–08 Premier League title was the most exciting in years. On the final day of the season, United were away at Wigan. If they won, they would be crowned champions. If they lost, Chelsea would be the winner instead.

Ryan sat on the subs bench and bit his nails. It was a very difficult game to watch, even when Wayne was fouled and Cristiano scored the penalty. With twenty minutes to go, Ryan came on and the United fans clapped loudly for their hero.

Giggsy! Giggsy! Giggsy!

In the nervous atmosphere, he almost forgot that

this was a special day: it was his 758th game for the club, which equalled the record set by Sir Bobby Charlton. Sir Bobby was watching the match from the directors' box and he clapped loudly.

With ten minutes left, United passed the ball around the pitch, looking for a second goal to secure the victory and the title. Wayne moved out to the left side and Ryan switched into the middle. It made life more difficult for the defenders.

When Wayne got the ball, Ryan knew exactly the right run to make to find space. The pass was perfect and he was in the penalty area. Ryan didn't rush. He took a touch and placed his shot past the goalkeeper.

Goooooooooooooooooaaaaaaaaaaaaaaaaaaaalllllllllllll llllllllllllllllll!!!!!!!!!!!!!!

What a moment! Ryan ran past all of the cheering supporters and slid along the grass. A few seconds later, he was at the bottom of a huge pile of players, including Edwin van der Sar, the goalkeeper. On the touchline, Ferguson danced with joy.

'Come on!' Ryan shouted to the fans as he made

his way back to his own half. He was about to win his tenth Premier League title.

As they celebrated after the game, Sir Bobby came on to the pitch to speak to Ryan.

'Congratulations, I'm so pleased that you'll be the one to break my record,' he said with tears in his eyes. 'What a player you are!'

It was a very emotional moment for both of them. Ryan had always looked up to Sir Bobby as a football legend and it was a real honour to follow in his footsteps.

Rio Ferdinand was the captain for the game but Fergie wanted Ryan to lift the trophy.

'It's your big day and it's your turn to have the glory!' he said and Rio agreed.

As he raised it into the air, Ryan's teammates joined him and they danced and sang. It was the best feeling in the world, another perfect day.

There was one game left in the season, however. In the Champions League, United faced Chelsea again in an all-English final.

'They'll be looking for revenge,' Fergie told his players. 'We have to be at our best.'

Again, Ryan watched from the sidelines for most of the game. He sat there in his shorts and socks, waiting for his opportunity. United took the lead through a Cristiano header but Frank Lampard equalised for Chelsea.

Near the end of the ninety minutes, Ryan came on for Scholesy. He was determined to make an impact. In extra time, Antonio ran down the right and pulled the ball back to Ryan near the edge of the penalty area. It was a brilliant chance to score the winner but John Terry made a great block.

Minutes later, the referee blew the final whistle and the match went to penalties. Ferguson needed to choose his first five takers. Ryan had a lot of experience but he had never taken many penalties. He wasn't surprised when he wasn't picked. He watched from the halfway line, ready to help his team if he was needed.

After ten penalties, it was a 4-4 draw. It went to sudden death and Ryan was United's second man. The walk to the penalty area seemed to take forever. As the rain poured down on his head, he focused on scoring. He had practised penalties in training and after so many years of success, he felt confident.

Ryan ran from the edge of the penalty area. In the heat of the moment, he stuck to his plan and aimed for the bottom right corner. It was where he always placed them but if he hit it low and hard enough, the keeper couldn't save it. Petr Čech dived the wrong way and the ball hit the back of the net.

Goooooooooooooaaaaaaaaaaaaaaaaaaaaalllllllllllllllll lllllllllllllllllllllllllll!!!!!!!!!!!!

'Yes, come on!' Ryan shouted to the United fans behind the goal. He was very relieved that he hadn't let his team down.

Edwin saved Chelsea's next penalty and United were the Champions of Europe. Ryan and his teammates sprinted towards their goalkeeper to celebrate.

'We've worked so hard this season,' he told them. 'Now it's time to enjoy it!'

This time, Rio and Ryan collected the trophy together. They kissed the silverware and lifted it high into the Moscow sky. It was another amazing moment in a long career of amazing moments.

CHAPTER 21

STILL GOING STRONG

TV presenter Jeff Stelling handed over to boxer Joe Calzaghe for the big announcement of the night: the PFA Player of the Year 2009.

Ryan was shocked to even make the shortlist. At the age of thirty-five, he had only started twelve matches in the Premier League all season but he was sure that one of his United teammates – Cristiano, Nemanja Vidič, Rio Ferdinand or Edwin van der Sar – would win the award. It was nice to be there at the fancy ceremony to see them collect the prize.

'In third place,' announced Joe Calzaghe, 'Nemanja Vidič of Manchester United.'

Everyone clapped.

'In second place, Steven Gerrard of Liverpool.'

Everyone clapped again. 'It must be Cristiano!'
Ryan thought to himself.

'In first place... he's not just my favourite player
but he's also Welsh like me, Ryan Giggs!'

Wow, it was the biggest personal honour in English
football and it had taken Ryan eighteen years to win
it. He was in shock as he walked up onto the stage.
He hugged Calzaghe and collected the trophy. Now,
for the hardest part: the speech.

Ryan was still a shy person and so speaking in front
of so many people was his worst nightmare. He was
nearly as nervous as the day when he met the Queen
to collect his OBE. When Elizabeth II pinned the gold
medal on his jacket, he could feel the sweat dripping
down his face.

At least this time Ryan was surrounded by football
people. He cleared his throat and started with a
tribute to his manager, Alex Ferguson: 'He's the
biggest influence on my career. I've known him since
I was thirteen and he knows me better than anyone.'

Next, he spoke about his grandpa, Dennis, who

was there at the event. 'He's supported me since I was nine or ten, so I'm really glad that he's here to see this!'

Jeff Stelling had a big question for Ryan. 'This year's Premier League title race – it's pretty much over, isn't it?'

Ryan smiled; he was used to answering this kind of question. 'No, there are still big games to go. But if we keep playing well, we should be okay.'

It was a very special moment as he stood there with the trophy and a Welsh choir sang 'Land of My Fathers'. But the next day, it was back to the training ground. Ryan had more trophies to win with United.

'Everyone's talking about me like my career is about to end,' he said to Gary. 'But I'm not going anywhere!'

Each year, people expected Ryan to run out of energy but he was still performing at the highest level for United. He couldn't play every game anymore but when his team needed a moment of magic, they could still rely on him.

Against West Ham, the match was goalless after

sixty minutes and United needed to win to return to
the top of the table. Scholesy passed to Ryan out on
the left wing. A defender slid in to make a tackle but
he cut inside. Another defender came across to block
him and Ryan pretended to shoot but cut inside again.
He was on his right foot but that wasn't a problem.
In the penalty area, he spotted the bottom corner and
aimed for it.

*Goooooooooooooooaaaaaaaaaaaaaaaaaaaaaaaaaalllll
lllllllllllllllllllllll!!!!!!!!!!!!!!!!!*

When Ryan won his eleventh Premier League title
with United, people asked the same old questions and
he gave the same old answers.

'I'm not ready to quit yet,' he told Wayne. 'Besides,
what would you do without me?'

Early in the 2009–10 season, Tottenham scored
within the first minute of the match. Ryan knew
that they didn't need to panic. Later in the first half,
United won a free kick. Wayne went to take it but he
dummied the ball. Ryan stepped up and curled the
ball into the top corner.

'What a strike!' Nemanja cheered.

Their next match was the Manchester derby. City had a new owner with lots of money and suddenly, the local rivalry was stronger than ever.

'We need to show them that we're still the best team in Manchester!' Ferguson said before kick-off and his players roared.

It was a very entertaining match. Every time United scored, City equalised. It was 3-3 with seconds to go. The United fans were desperate for a winner.

Attack! Attack! Attack!

Wayne kept putting the ball in the box but United needed their calmest player on the ball. To win the derby, they needed something clever, something special. The ball fell to Ryan about forty yards from goal. He had already spotted Michael Owen in space on the left side of the penalty area. The pass would have to be perfect and so Ryan took his time.

Michael was in and he poked the ball past the keeper. 4-3! Ryan had rarely heard so much noise at Old Trafford. Ferguson ran along the touchline celebrating, while the players pumped their fists at the crowd.

'Unbelievable!' Ryan shouted at the final whistle. 'That must be the best Manchester derby ever.'

'And we have you to thank for the victory,' Michael said, giving him a big hug. 'Giggsy to the rescue yet again!'

CHAPTER 22

STILL MORE TO OFFER

'All I've ever wanted to do is play for United,' Ryan told the media as he signed another one-year contract. 'I've been lucky enough to do that for twenty years, and I think I've still got more to offer.'

Ferguson was delighted. Gary had just retired, so Ryan and Scholesy were the only players left from the 'Class of '92'. With United bringing through lots of exciting new young players, it was very important for them to learn from experienced professionals.

'Some of these kids weren't even born when I started playing for the club!' Ryan joked but he enjoyed his role as a mentor.

In the opening match of the 2010–11 season

against Newcastle, Scholesy played one of his classic long passes to the left side of the penalty area. After all those years playing together, he knew exactly where Ryan would be.

Ryan had scored many volleys in his career and he didn't wait for Scholesy's pass to bounce. His shot thundered into the bottom corner.

Goooooooooooooooooooooaaaaaaaaaaaaaaaaaalllllllllllll lllllllllllllllllll!!!!!!!!!!

Ryan went to thank his teammate for the assist. They high-fived and hugged each other.

'I can relax now,' Ryan said. 'I've still scored in every Premier League season!'

Yet again, United were aiming for the Treble. Ryan didn't play in the FA Cup semi-final defeat to local rivals Manchester City but he was back for the Champions League semi-final against Schalke 04.

'I wouldn't miss a big European night for the world,' he told Ferguson. The fire still burned in his eyes – he loved battling and winning.

Away in Germany, United played brilliantly but

their goalkeeper Manuel Neuer saved every shot. Some of the players were getting frustrated but not Ryan.

'The goal will come,' he told them at half-time, and they, of course, believed him.

The goal did come and it was Ryan himself who scored it. Wayne dropped deep to pick up the ball. Three Schalke defenders circled him and they left a big gap behind them. Ryan knew where to run and Wayne knew where to pass. They had been a great partnership for years.

Ryan knew that Neuer was a brilliant shot-stopper, so he decided to shoot as early as possible before the keeper could get himself ready to dive. He also decided to take a risk. He fired the ball straight through Neuer's legs and into the net. Nutmeg!

Goooooooooooooooooaaaaaaaaaaaaaaaaalllllllllllllllllllll llllllll!!!!!!!!!!!!!!!!!!!

Wayne made it 2-0 a few minutes later and United were on the verge of another European Final.

'Congratulations!' Scholesy said to Ryan at the final whistle.

'Thanks, it was nice to get on the scoresheet again,' he replied.

'Has no-one told you yet?' Scholesy asked with a big smile on his face.

Ryan had no idea what his friend was talking about. 'Told me what?'

Scholesy burst out laughing. 'You're going to love this – you're now the oldest goalscorer in Champions League history!'

Ryan didn't like to be reminded about his age but he could see the funny side of it. 'I can't stop breaking records these days!'

With Premier League title number twelve in the bag, Ryan couldn't wait for the European final. United were up against Barcelona, who had beaten them in the 2009 final in Rome. It had been the worst moment of Ryan's career and he had even thought about retiring afterwards. But instead he had carried on playing and it was now time for revenge.

'If we win, only Paolo Maldini and Alessandro Costacurta and Clarence Seedorf will have more winner's medals than us!' he told Scholesy.

As the Champions League anthem filled Wembley stadium, Ryan felt the adrenaline running through his body. At the age of thirty-seven, he was still playing on the biggest stage.

United started well but Lionel Messi, Xavi and Andrés Iniesta were just too good. They passed and passed and passed until they scored. Ryan worked hard and set up Wayne's equaliser with a great one-two, but there was nothing he could do as Messi and David Villa made it 3-1.

At the final whistle, some of the younger players lay down on the grass and cried. Ryan was disappointed too but he went to speak to them.

'We did ourselves proud out there tonight. Don't be too upset – we just got beaten by the best team in the world.'

Ryan hoped that he would have more big European nights but it might only take one more injury to end his incredible career. As he walked off the pitch, he promised to enjoy every moment of football while it lasted.

In June 2012, Ryan was back at Wembley but he

wasn't playing for Manchester United and he wasn't playing for Wales either. For the London Olympic Games, Great Britain had put together a special team to represent England, Scotland, Wales and Northern Ireland. The Team GB manager, Stuart Pearce, could only select three players who were older than twenty-three, and Ryan was top of his list.

'Giggsy, I really want you to be my captain. We've got a lot of young players and they need an experienced leader. You'll be perfect!'

Ryan thought about the offer and decided to say yes. It was a great chance to finally take part in a major international football tournament. Other top-class players had turned out for the Olympics in previous years: Ronaldo had played for Brazil in 1996 and Lionel Messi had played for Argentina in 2008. Now, Ryan could be the star of 2012.

Against the United Arab Emirates, Craig Bellamy got the ball on the left wing and looked up to see who was in the box. Ryan had made a brilliant run to the back post and he headed the cross down into the bottom corner. The goalkeeper could only stand and watch the ball hit the back of the net.

Goooooooooooooooooooooaaaaaaaaaaaaaaaaaalllllllll lllllllllllllllllll!!!!!!!!!!!!!!!

It was a great feeling to score for Team GB and he pumped his fist at the crowd. At thirty-eight, he was still entertaining the fans.

Ryan was injured for the win over Uruguay and he was a late substitute in the quarter-final against South Korea, held in Cardiff. After extra time, the match went to penalties. As captain, Ryan knew that he had to take one.

'Come on, boys!' he shouted, as his teammates rested on the grass. 'You've seen how well the other Team GB athletes are doing – we need to make the UK proud!'

When Ryan stepped up to take Team GB's fourth penalty, the score was 3-3. The pressure was on but he was fearless. He took a long run-up from outside the penalty area and by the time he reached the ball, the goalkeeper was already diving to his left. So Ryan placed it perfectly in the opposite corner.

Unfortunately, Daniel Sturridge's subsequent penalty was saved and Team GB were knocked out of the tournament. Ryan had enjoyed his Olympic experience but it was disappointing to miss out on the semi-finals.

'I think I'm cursed when it comes to international football,' Ryan told Craig as they walked off the pitch in Cardiff.

Craig smiled. 'Maybe, but your club career has been pretty amazing!'

CHAPTER 23

A FOND FAREWELL

In May 2013, the football world received some shocking news. After twenty-six incredible years at Old Trafford, Sir Alex Ferguson was retiring as Manchester United manager. It was very sad news for all United fans but it was particularly sad news for Ryan.

'I just can't believe it,' he said to Scholesy. 'I can't imagine this club without Fergie!'

Only a few weeks earlier, United had celebrated yet another Premier League title, the thirteenth of Ryan's career. He owed so much of his success to his manager, who had always been a father figure to him. If he ever needed help or advice, Fergie was always the person that he spoke to.

The news made Ryan think about retirement too. He already had his coaching badges and he was looking ahead to a career in management. Was there anything left to achieve? He had played over 900 matches for his childhood club, winning thirty-four trophies. Each year, he asked himself if he had the fitness and desire to keep playing, and every year he said yes. But eventually, he would have to say no.

'You can't stop yet!' Wayne begged him. 'We're going to have a new manager and we'll need the winning experience that you and Scholesy have more than ever.'

When David Moyes was announced as the new United manager, one of the first things he did was speak to Ryan.

'Giggsy, you've got a very important role to play this season, both on and off the pitch,' Moyes told him. 'I want you to keep playing but I also want you to join the coaching staff.'

Ryan thought about the offer and decided that it was the right thing to do. The last thing he wanted to do was let his beloved club down. He would play for one more season.

'Let's show Fergie that we can carry on his legacy!' Ryan told his teammates. Youngsters Tom Cleverley and Danny Welbeck were carrying on the tradition of local talent.

The season started well, as United won the Charity Shield and their first Premier League match. But soon, life after Fergie became very difficult. United lost 4-1 in the Manchester derby and by March 2014, they were seventh in the Premier League with very little chance of qualifying for Europe.

'This is terrible!' the players complained after a 2-0 defeat to Moyes' old club, Everton. 'We've got the same team as last season but we're not playing well at all.'

When Moyes was sacked in April, there was only one man that everyone wanted to take over the job for the rest of the season.

'Give it to Giggsy!' the fans cheered.

Ryan was used to dealing with the pressures of life at the biggest club in the world. He was Mr

Manchester United. It would be a tough job, even for four games, but Ryan had the support of a lot of people, including Fergie.

'I promise to do the best job possible,' he told the media when the news was announced.

Ryan was very nervous before his first match as manager but he had no need to worry – United thrashed Norwich 4-0.

'What a start, boss!' Wayne joked at the final whistle.

But in the next match, the team lost 1-0 to Sunderland at home. Ryan found it very frustrating to watch from the sidelines. Once his players went out on to the pitch, there wasn't much that he could do to help.

United's last match at Old Trafford in the 2013–14 season was against Hull. It would be Ryan's final home game as manager and also his final home game as a player. After twenty-four seasons, his United adventure was nearly over.

'I hope I'm not making a mistake,' he said to his mum.

'I think the time has finally come to hang up that Number 11 shirt,' Lynne replied. She knew that it would be a very emotional day for her son.

Ryan gave striker James Wilson his debut and he scored two goals. With twenty minutes left, he brought himself on. The United fans sang his name at the top of their lungs.

Giggsy! Giggsy! Giggsy!

Could there be a fairytale ending to his fairytale career? United won a free kick and Ryan had his chance. He curled the ball up over the wall and it was heading for the top left corner, but the goalkeeper made a brilliant save. Ryan smiled – not this time.

At the final whistle, Ryan made a speech on the pitch. He thanked the fans and talked about the exciting times ahead for the club. He could feel the tears building in his eyes.

For Ryan, an incredible journey had come to an end. He had so many people to thank – his family who had always supported him, his friends who had helped to keep his feet on the ground, and the youth coaches who had spotted his talent.

And of course, there was everyone at Manchester United: all of the coaches, all of the teammates and that one brilliant manager, Sir Alex Ferguson. Ryan had come so far from his debut in 1991 to this moment in 2014. In between, he had won thirteen Premier League titles, four FA Cup trophies and two Champions League trophies.

At Manchester United, Ryan had become a wing wizard and the most successful British footballer ever. It was hard to explain how much the club and its supporters meant to him.

A couple of weeks later, he wrote an open letter to them:

'It's so difficult to say goodbye after twenty-nine years at this club. I have loved every minute of it. Your support has always been phenomenal, thank you.'

Turn the page for a sneak preview of
another brilliant football story by
Matt and Tom Oldfield. . .

ALEXIS SÁNCHEZ

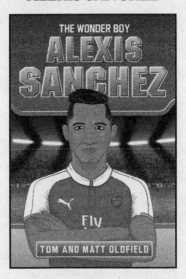

Available now!

CHAPTER 1

WINNING AT WEMBLEY

'*Alexis Sánchez baby, Alexis Sánchez
oooohhhhhhhh!*'

Alexis could hear the Arsenal fans loud and clear as he warmed up on the Wembley pitch. He loved the song that they had made for him. There was still half an hour until kick-off but the atmosphere was already amazing. It was Arsenal's second FA Cup Final in a row but for Alexis, this was the chance to win a first English trophy, and what a trophy it was. Even as a kid growing up in Chile, Alexis knew about the oldest football competition in the world. It was a dream come true.

'Alexis, this is it,' Arsène Wenger said to him in the

dressing room before the game, but he knew he didn't really need to inspire his superstar. 'You've had an amazing first year here but you need to end it with a winner's medal!'

As Alexis walked out on to the pitch, holding the hand of a mascot, fireworks went off all over the pitch. The FA Cup trophy was sitting there, shining brightly and waiting for him. He couldn't wait to get the ball and run at the Aston Villa defence. He knew it would be a tough game but there was no way he was going to lose this match. Alexis had been the Arsenal hero in the semi-final, scoring both goals to beat Reading. And he was determined to be the hero again in the final.

'We need to stay focused and we need to be patient,' Alexis said to Mesut Özil and Theo Walcott, his partners in attack. 'If we play well, we will score in the end.'

Alexis was right. Aston Villa stopped them again and again but the Gunners didn't give up or get frustrated. At the end of the first half, the Gunners finally scored and it was thanks to Alexis. Nacho

Monreal crossed from the left and Alexis was there at the back post. He couldn't get enough power to head for goal so instead he headed the ball across to Theo, who smashed it into the back of the net. They had that goal they needed.

'I'm not done yet,' Alexis told Mesut once Arsène had given his half-time team talk. The important message was that they were only halfway to victory. 'I want to win but I also want to score!'

Five minutes into the second half, Alexis chased across the pitch to get to the ball first. The Aston Villa defenders backed away in fear of what he might do with his brilliant skill. Alexis had the space he needed for one of his trademark long-range shots. With his right foot, he hit the ball with so much power and swerve that the goalkeeper could do nothing as it sailed over his head. Alexis couldn't believe it; he had scored and it was one of his best goals ever.

Per Mertesacker scored a third and Olivier Giroud made it four. 4–0 – what a way to win the FA Cup Final! On the touchline, Arsène clapped and allowed himself to smile. He was very proud of his squad and

especially his Chilean superstar. What a signing he
had been.

'*Arsenal! Arsenal! Arsenal!*' Alexis shouted with
his teammates at the final whistle. They were a close
group of friends and they were in the mood for a
party.

With an Arsenal scarf around his neck and a
Chilean flag in his hands, Alexis was one of the first
players to walk up the stadium steps to collect his
medal from Prince William. As he passed, the fans
high-fived him and patted him on the back. He was
part of the Arsenal family now and he loved it. It was
great to get the medal but what he really wanted was
the trophy. Captains Per and Mikel Arteta were the
first to lift it and then it was his turn.

Alexis shouted for joy as he raised it above his head.
He kissed it twice and passed it on to Jack Wilshere.

'We did it!' Jack told him, giving him a big hug. He
was wearing a silly red-and-white jester hat and he
was having the time of his life.

It wasn't Alexis's first trophy but it was certainly
one of his favourites. Down on the pitch, there

GIGGS

were more fireworks and Theo sprayed champagne everywhere. The players thanked the fans by having selfies taken with them. It was a really great celebration. Alexis wished that his family and friends could have come from Chile to share his special day but they had all sent him good-luck messages.

It was an incredible way to end the best season of his career so far. Twenty-five goals and twelve assists was a new record for Alexis. The big-money transfer from Barcelona had put a lot of pressure on him to perform. He had worked really hard and the players and fans had made him feel so welcome. Arsenal Football Club felt like home and he was already excited about challenging for more trophies next year.

'Let's win the Premier League *and* the Champions League!' Alexis told Mesut as they posed for more photos.

He had come a long way from Tocopilla.

RYAN GIGGS HONOURS

Manchester United

- 🏆 Premier League: 1992–93, 1993–94, 1995–96, 1996–97, 1998–99, 1999–2000, 2000–01, 2002–03, 2006–07, 2007–08, 2008–09, 2010–11, 2012–13
- 🏆 FA Cup: 1993–94, 1995–96, 1998–99, 2003–04
- 🏆 League Cup: 1991–92, 2005–06, 2008–09, 2009–10
- 🏆 UEFA Champions League: 1998–99, 2007–08
- 🏆 FIFA Club World Cup: 2008

Individual

- 🏆 PFA Young Player of the Year: 1991–92, 1992–93
- 🏆 PFA Premier League Team of the Year: 1992–93,

1997–98, 2000–01, 2001–02, 2006–07, 2008–09

🏆 Wales Player of the Year Award: 1996, 2006

🏆 BBC Goal of the Season: 1998–99

🏆 PFA Players' Player of the Year: 2008–09

🏆 BBC Sports Personality of the Year: 2009

GIGGS

⑪ THE FACTS

NAME:
Ryan Joseph Giggs

DATE OF BIRTH:
29 November 1973

AGE: 43

PLACE OF BIRTH:
Canton, Cardiff

NATIONALITY: Wales

BEST FRIENDS: The Class of 92

CLUB: Manchester United

POSITION: LW

THE STATS

Height (cm):	**179**
Club appearances:	**963**
Club goals:	**168**
Club trophies:	**35**
International appearances:	**64**
International goals:	**12**
International trophies:	**0**
Ballon d'Ors:	**0**

★ ★ ★ **HERO RATING: 90** ★ ★ ★

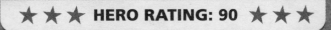

GREATEST MOMENTS

Type and search the web links to see the magic for yourself!

4 MAY 1991, MANCHESTER UNITED 1-0 MANCHESTER CITY

https://www.youtube.com/watch?v=OdkXPZgb7N4
Two months after making his first-team debut,
Ryan started in the Manchester Derby. He was only
seventeen and he scored his first ever goal. Or so he
claimed, anyway. Brian McClair's cross seemed to go
in off the defender Colin Hendry but Ryan celebrated
anyway. It was the winning goal and the start of
great things at Old Trafford.

6 APRIL 1996, MANCHESTER CITY 2-3 MANCHESTER UNITED

https://www.youtube.com/watch?v=ujYfIXuEbv0
This was the season that the 'Class of 92' stormed the Premier League. Ryan was the oldest and most experienced of the group. As they chased the title, United needed a win in the Manchester Derby but it was 2-2 with 15 minutes to go. When Ryan got the ball, he didn't dribble as he usually did. Instead, he struck a brilliant shot into the top corner.

14 APRIL 1999, MANCHESTER UNITED 2-1 ARSENAL

https://www.youtube.com/watch?v=quI_LkMj4HI
This may be the greatest goal in English football history. In extra-time in the FA Cup semi-final replay, Ryan got the ball in his own half and dribbled forward. He went past Patrick Vieira, then Lee Dixon, and then dribbled between two more defenders. Ryan completed his wondergoal by shooting over David Seaman and into the roof of the net.

26 MAY 1999, MANCHESTER UNITED 2-1 BAYERN MUNICH

https://www.youtube.com/watch?v=XjxHp2A5BsU
Ryan didn't score in the Champions League final but he still played an important role. In the 91st minute, he took a shot from the edge of the penalty area and Teddy Sheringham steered the ball into the net. 1-1! Manchester United went on to win 2-1 and secure an incredible Treble.

21 MAY 2008, MANCHESTER UNITED 1-1 CHELSEA (6-5 ON PENALTIES)

https://www.youtube.com/watch?v=h2f3Vdn1u8U
As Ryan got older, he played fewer games for Manchester United. However, Sir Alex Ferguson still needed his talent and experience. In the 2008 Champions League Final, Ryan came on in the 87th minute. He held his nerve and scored in the penalty shoot-out. Ryan added a second Champions League trophy to his massive collection.

PLAY LIKE YOUR HEROES

THE RYAN GIGGS
WONDER DRIBBLE

SEE IT HERE YouTube

https://www.youtube.com/watch?v=quI_LkMj4HI

STEP 1: Run forward and watch the defenders back away. You're the best dribbler around and everyone knows it!

STEP 2: Stay light on your toes so you can shift your body quickly from side to side.

STEP 3: Wait for the first defender's tackle. At the last moment, shift the ball to the left and then sprint away.

STEP 4: Run towards goal, weaving from side to side like you're dribbling through cones, to confuse defenders.

STEP 5: As the defenders close in on you, tap the ball from your left foot to your right foot and back again as fast as you can. They won't be able to stop you.

TEST YOUR KNOWLEDGE

QUESTIONS

1. How old was Ryan when his family moved from Cardiff to Manchester?

2. Who was Ryan's childhood Manchester United hero?

3. How old was Ryan when he chose football over rugby?

4. Ryan trained with Manchester City before Manchester United – true or false?

5. Which Manchester United legend was Ryan often compared to?

6. How old was Ryan when he changed his surname from Wilson to Giggs?

7. Who challenged Ryan to a 'Loudest Jacket' competition in May 1993?

8. What position did Ryan play in the 1999 Champions League final and why?

9. What did Ryan start doing in his thirties to help him play football for longer?

10. Which year did Ryan win PFA Player of the Year?

11. Which club did Ryan make his final Manchester United appearance against?

Answers below. . . No cheating!

1. *Six* 2. *Mickey Thomas* 3. *Thirteen* 4. *True - but Ryan wore a red shirt to his first session! Luckily United stoon stole him away.* 5. *George Best* 6. *Sixteen* 7. *Paul Ince* 8. *He played right-wing, because David Beckham was moved to central midfield.* 9. *Yoga* 10. *2009* 11. *Hull City*

HAVE YOU GOT THEM ALL?

ULTIMATE FOOTBALL HEROES